A CONTEMPORARY READING

OF THE

SPIRITUAL EXERCISES

This book is Number 2 in

Series IV: Study Aids on Jesuit Topics

DAVID L. FLEMING, S.J.

A CONTEMPORARY READING

OF THE

SPIRITUAL EXERCISES

A Companion to St. Ignatius' Text

Experimental Edition

THE INSTITUTE OF JESUIT SOURCES

St. Louis, 1976

IMPRIMI POTEST: Very Reverend Leo F. Weber, S.J.
                 Provincial of the Missouri Province
                 January 15, 1976

IMPRIMATUR: Most Reverend George J. Gottwald
                 Vicar General of St. Louis
                 January 19, 1976

Published through the aid of funds

donated by the late Mr. James L. Monaghan

of Milwaukee, Wisconsin,

1867 - 1963,

in memory of his brother,

Reverend Edward V. Monaghan, S.J.,

1879 - 1922.

CONTENTS

ON SERIES IV: STUDY AIDS ON JESUIT TOPICS

The Institute of Jesuit Sources is happy to offer the present
book by Father David L. Fleming, S.J., <u>A Contemporary Reading of</u>
<u>the Spiritual Exercises: A Companion to St. Ignatius' Text</u>, as
Number 2 in its Series IV: Study Aids on Jesuit Topics. It is
being published first in an experimental edition because the au-
thor hopes to receive comments from his readers which will help
him in the eventual preparation of a revision.

It seems advisable to state the rationale of Series IV in
each volume published in it. The series is an effort to solve
various aspects of the following problem.

From its inception the Institute of Jesuit Sources has been
oriented toward the publishing of scholarly books of quality. Such
books, carefully selected, obviously have advantages, especially the
long-lasting values arising from their presence in libraries. But
this orientation, if maintained exclusively, also entails two disadvantages which are especially hampering and costly in our present
era of rapid developments and changes: the lengthy time required
for the writing and editing, and the expense of typesetting, print-
ing, and binding with cloth.

There is another class of writings, such as doctoral disserta-
tions, study aids, bibliographies, monographs, preliminary editions,
and documented or well founded reflections, which have a different
but genuine value. These are, in many cases, not yet the finished,
polished, and fully matured scholarship ordinarily found in the
volumes published by university presses. But they are a step toward

such scholarship. They contain much sound material which is truly
helpful to interested persons and which would remain unavailable if
postponed until high perfection could be attained. In many cases
such delay could all too easily turn out to be an instance in which
the dreamed of best, which may never come, is the enemy which defeats
the presently attainable good.

This new Series IV will consist of studies in this category.
Hopefully, too, it will offer some solution of the problem sketched
above. An effort will be made to keep the books or booklets inex-
pensive through the use of typewriter composition and paperback
bindings. Editorial time and cost, too, will be kept as low as
possible, with the responsibility for details being allowed to rest
more fully on the authors than on the editors of the Institute of
Jesuit Sources.

In the designing of this new series, many helpful ideas have
been taken from the somewhat similar procedure in scholarly publishing which has been launched by the Council on the Study of
Religion, for example, in the two "Dissertation Series" respectively
of the American Academy of Religion and of the Society of Biblical
Literature. The rationale of these series is well described by
Robert W. Funk and Robert A. Spivey in the Bulletin for the Council
on the Study of Religion, Volume IV, number 3 (June, 1973), pages
3-13, 28-29, and 36-37; and also, at greater length, in the Report
of the Task Force on Scholarly Communication and Publication, edited
by George W. MacRae, S.J. (1972, available from the Council on the
Study of Religion Executive Office, Waterloo Lutheran University,
Waterloo, Ontario, Canada). Indebtedness to this helpful information and example is gratefully acknowledged.

George E. Ganss, S.J.
Director and General Editor
The Institute of Jesuit Sources

The present small book is intended to be a gateway to St.
Ignatius' Spiritual Exercises, a means to make his widely renowned
but difficult text more easily and quickly understood by contemporary
men and women--especially by those using it for the first time in
directed retreats.

The Spiritual Exercises of the founder of the Jesuits has been
a classic retreat manual in the tradition of the Church for the past
four hundred years. Spiritual classics, of their very nature, are
not meant to be rewritten or tampered with.

Yet significant contributions to the understanding of the Exercises and its application in practice have been made throughout
the centuries since their publication in 1548. During Ignatius' own
lifetime and for the first fifty years after his death, various commentaries on the text of the Exercises were written which looked
primarily to the actual practice in giving the Exercises. After
the official Directory of the Spiritual Exercises was promulgated
by the Society of Jesus in 1599, there was something of a lull in
this style of writing. But soon commentaries of different types--
some more in the nature of theological explanation of the text,
others still practice-oriented in terms of particular movements or
devotions in the Church--were forthcoming. In our own more recent
past, retreat manuals were written in which the conferences of a
preached-style retreat were put into print so that they could both
inspire other directors and help other retreatants. These books
provided a certain understanding of the Exercises, and they also
at times gave direction through the written word to those who made
use of them for their own private retreats.

Today, the popularity of the directed retreat has led directors
and retreatants back to the starkness of the original Ignatian text.
But the text itself, despite a simplicity in style, presents difficulties in word expression, image patterns, terminology, and even in
the more medieval outlook of his world view. Often the director and
retreatant of today spend time on technicalities of the text when
such time could be better employed in the movement of the retreat
itself. I believe that what might be helpful to men of our times
would be an attempt to preserve the original sparseness of the Ignatian text, yet to express it in such a way that the book seems
not quite so formidable for either the present-day director or the
retreatant. I would hope that the director would find such a re-
expression of the Ignatian text enlightening and opening out to
new depths of understanding. In a similar way, it is my desire to
be able to provide a reading which the director would find is less
forbidding in terminology and less tortuous in explanation when he
wants to put the text in the hands of a retreatant. In other words,
I want to present the text in a way that it is as easily usable and
understandable for people today as Ignatius' text was for the men
of his time.

This, then, is why I entitle my efforts "a contemporary reading
of the Spiritual Exercises." It is not a translation in the more
usual sense of the word since I am not struggling with a rendering
of the Spanish or Latin versions. Even though I have at times ex-
panded and re-arranged some parts of the text, I do not want it to
be considered a commentary or a substitute for the text of Ignatius.
Because this work is a way of "reading" the text of Ignatius, I hope
that it will always draw a person back to the original source which
must remain the incentive and guide for the full movement of the
retreat. In order to facilitate the movement between this "reading"
and the original text of Ignatius, I have placed in brackets throughout the text the system of numbering which is used to identify paragraphs of the Spiritual Exercises in all modern editions, including
that in Exercitia Spiritualia: Textus (Rome: Institutum Historicum
Societatis Iesu, 1969), the authoritative edition found in the series

Monumenta Historica Societatis Jesu. I have called this book an "experimental edition" because, through usage by many people, I hope that directors and retreatants will help me, by their own criticisms and suggestions, to form a more adequate text. I look forward to reader reaction. Letters may be sent to me at The Institute of Jesuit Sources, 3700 West Pine Boulevard, St. Louis, Missouri 63108.

I feel that what I share with my readers is the compilation of those ideas which many others have passed along to me--either in writings or in conversation or in the experiences of a retreat. My desire is that what I have been given, digested, and found helpful may be found helpful and encouraging to others too, and also supportive of their own efforts both to understand the Exercises and to make them come alive for the retreatant.

To enter into the mind and spirit of St. Ignatius is the desire of everyone who directs retreats according to the manner of his Spiritual Exercises. No one of us, of course, can do so fully. But it is necessary that the legacy which he left to the Church and to the Society of Jesus should be made to live on with all the passion and power which he gave to it. I pray that St. Ignatius will favor and guide this latest attempt to open up his Exercises for the men and women of our times.

David L. Fleming, S.J.

A CONTEMPORARY READING

OF THE

SPIRITUAL EXERCISES

THE PRAYER "SOUL OF CHRIST"

Jesus, may all that is you flow into me.

May your body and blood be my food and drink.

May your passion and death be my strength and life.

Jesus, with you by my side enough has been given.

May the shelter I seek be the shadow of your cross.

Let me not run from the love which you offer,

But hold me safe from the forces of evil.

On each of my dyings shed your light and your love.

Keep calling to me until that day comes,

When, with your saints, I may praise you forever.

Amen.

SOME PRELIMINARY HELPS

(from the reading of

the Spiritual Exercises, [1-20]*)

The purpose of these observations is to provide some
understanding of the spiritual exercises which follow
and to serve as a help both for the retreatant and for
the director of the retreat.

A. For the Retreatant

1, (Spiritual Exercises, [1]). The phrase "Spiritual Exercises"
takes in all the ways we have of making formal contact with God, such
as meditation, contemplation, vocal prayer, devotions, examination of
conscience, and so on. We are familiar with the great variety of
physical exercises, such as walking, jogging, playing games such as
tennis, handball, golf, or even the demands of yoga and isometrics.
These physical exercises are good for tuning up muscles, improving
circulation and breathing, and in general for the overall good health
of the body. So, too, what we call Spiritual Exercises are good for
increasing openness to the movement of the Spirit, for helping to
bring to light the darknesses of sinfulness and sinful tendencies
within a man, and for strengthening and supporting him in the effort
to respond ever more faithfully to the love of God.

2, (Spiritual Exercises, [3]). In all the Spiritual Exercises
which follow, we find ourselves sometimes doing a lot of thinking and
reasoning things out. At other times, we experience far more the

---

* The numbers enclosed within square brackets refer, throughout
this book, to the paragraph numbers found in most modern editions
of The Spiritual Exercises of St. Ignatius of Loyola, which was
first published in 1548. These numbers were first added to his
text in the edition published at Turin in 1928, in order to make
references easier. In this book by Father Fleming, Spiritual
Exercises in italics refers chiefly to Ignatius' book, Spiritual
Exercises in roman type to the activities within a retreat.

response of our hearts, with little or nothing for the head to be concerned about. It is good to remember that we are always in the context of prayer, whether meditative or affective, and so we should always try to maintain a spirit of deep reverence before God.

3, [5]. The most important quality in the person who enters into these Exercises is openness and generosity. The retreatant's one hope and desire is that he can really put himself at the disposal of God so that in all ways he seeks only to respond to that love which first created him and now wraps him round with total care and concern.

4, [20]. Ordinarily, if we want to give ourselves over to the movement of these Exercises, it is most helpful to go apart from what usually surrounds us--both friends and family, job and recreation, and our usual places of home and work. There are many advantages which come from this separation, for example: 1) if one is so intent on responding ever better to the love of God wherever it will lead him in his life, he will find the kind of quiet in which the movement of God in his life becomes all the more apparent; 2) his mind will not find itself divided over many cares, but rather its one concern will be to follow the lead of God; 3) in a similar way, his powers of loving, too, are focused for this amount of time solely upon God, and the response which he will be able to make is all the more intense and intimate because the demand for such a response is so single.

5, [4]. The makeup of the Exercises is rather simple. The basic division is into four parts, called "Weeks," although there are no fixed number of days with such "weeks." The First Week is set in the context of God's love and its rejection by man in sin. The Second Week centers on the life of Jesus, from its beginnings through his public ministry. The Third Week fixes upon that very special time of Jesus' life--his passion and death. The Fourth Week looks upon the Risen Christ and the world which has been renewed in his victory.

A person moves from week to week according to the grace which God gives to him. Some come to an appreciation of a certain mystery of God's dealing with man more rapidly than others. For each person, it is the director who determines whether the time of the Week should be shortened or lengthened according to the movements of God's grace and a man's ability to respond. We note, however, that the full Exercises should be completed in approximately thirty days.

6, [11]. When a retreatant is involved with the exercises of the First Week, he should not try to escape from total attention upon those considerations by looking to the areas of the later Weeks. At each stage of the retreat, he should work as if his whole response to God is found in the matter at hand.

7, [12]. The one making the Exercises should ordinarily spend one full hour for each formal prayer period suggested by the director. When he feels tempted to cut short the hour, he should recognize the temptation for what it is--the first steps of taking back from God his total gift--and extend the time of prayer for a few minutes beyond the set time.

8, [13]. When one finds prayer a joy, he may well be tempted so to prolong the period of prayer that soon he finds himself responding to the consolations of God more than to God himself. At such times, the observance of the set hour is a safeguard against subtle self-seeking even in prayer. When one finds prayer dry and even a burden, he must be sure to spend the full hour as part of his attempt to respond by waiting on the Lord.

9, [16]. If the retreatant feels a disorder in his attachment to a person, to a job or position, to a certain religious house, a certain city, country, and so on, he should take it to the Lord and pray insistently to be given the grace to free himself from such

disorder. What he wants above all is the ability to respond freely
to God, and all other loves for people, places, and things are held
in proper perspective by the light and strength of God's grace.

10, [17]. The retreatant should be aware that the director,
even if a priest, is not necessarily one's confessor. It is not
essential for the director to know one's past sins or even his present
state of sin. At the same time, however, the attempt to speak out
one's temptations and fears, the consolations and lights given one
by God, the various movements that happen within one, is the great
advantage of a directed retreat, wherein the director can listen,
sometimes enlighten, and adapt the progress of the retreat according
to the way one is being led and is responding to God. Without this
openness between the retreatant and the director, the retreat itself
will not be able to be adapted and focused so as to lead to the growth
which is possible for the retreatant.

B. For the Director

1, [2]. The director's role is that of helper. He helps by
explaining the different ways of praying. He helps by suggesting
the matter to be considered in prayer, and he does not hinder God's
movements in the retreatant by imposing his own interpretations of
scripture or of theology. The Exercises are, above all, a time for
intimate contact between God and the retreatant, and the retreatant
will profit far more from the understanding and love aroused by the
grace of God than from the rhetoric or brilliance of the retreat
director.

2, [6]. The director should expect that in the course of a
Week the retreatant will be moved in various ways. When the retreatant claims that nothing is happening in his prayer, the director should ask how he goes about his prayer, at what times he
prays, where he prays, and in general how he spends the day. Sometimes what appears to be an action or event of small consequence can

affect the course of prayer for a whole day or a number of days. This again is an area where the director can be a great help by the kind of questioning which may uncover the cause that blocks the openness to God's call.

3, [7]. When the retreatant is in a time of temptation or desolation, the director should be a kind listener and gentle support. To the best of his ability, the director should help to expose the ways in which the powers of evil attempt to block the retreatant's ability to respond to God. He should remind the retreatant that God continues to be at hand even at such times with the necessary grace of strength and light.

4, [8]. As the retreatant begins to be aware of the various movements in himself, whether of consolation or desolation, the director should determine when it would be helpful to explain further the ways for discerning the sources of such movement so that the retreatant is better able to understand how to respond to God.

5, [9]. Since there are different sets of instructions about the way we are moved in the First Week in distinction to the Second Week and thereafter, the director should be careful to present and explain only what is more immediately helpful to the retreatant for where he is at present in his retreat. Otherwise, confusion can result from the very explanations which were meant to be a help.

6, [10]. In the First Week, it often happens that the retreatant will be tempted to discouragement or rejection by thoughts about his own unworthiness before God, the costs of such a loving response, or fear for what others might think or say of him. The director will find the Guidelines for the Discernment of Spirits for the First Week (p. 82 ff) helpful to present at this time. By contrast, in the Second Week, the temptation which the retreatant often faces comes more from the appeal and attraction of some good, real or apparent. At this time, the director will find the Guidelines for the

Discernment of Spirits for the Second Week (p. 87 below) more helpful.

7, [14]. The director should be cautious when a retreatant is uplifted by consolation or fervor so that he desires to make great plans or to pronounce some sort of vow. While the director should respect idealism, he must be able to weigh the gifts of God, along with the natural endowments of personality, character, and intelligence, as he works with the retreatant.

8, [15]. The director must always provide the balance for a retreatant, both in times of exhilaration and in times of discouragement. The director himself is not the one who should urge a particular decision--for example, to enter religious life, to marry this or that person, or to take a vow of poverty. The effort of the director is always to facilitate the movement of God's grace within the retreatant so that the light and love of God inflame all possible decisions and resolutions about life situations. The director should always remember that God is not only Creator but truly the Director of this person's retreat; the director himself should never provide a hindrance to such an intimate communication.

9, [18]. It is the role of the director to adapt the Spiritual Exercises to each retreatant, in view of his age and maturity, his education, and also his potential and his talents. The director should decide what exercises would prove useless or even harmful to a retreatant because of a lack of physical strength or natural ability as well as what exercises would benefit and perhaps challenge a retreatant who is properly disposed and endowed. The director may often discover that a retreatant at this particular time of life has neither the ability nor sometimes the desire to go beyond what is ordinarily described as the exercises of the First Week. So, too, the director should make the judgment whether the full Exercises would be profitable to a particular retreatant at this time. Because the Exercises are a limited instrument through which God can work, the director should be aware that many persons would not be able to enter well into the Exercises, perhaps because of a lack of natural talents, perhaps because of a certain kind of personality, or perhaps because God does not draw them to respond through the structured method of these Exercises.

10, [19]. A director may want to help a retreatant of talent and proper disposition through the full Exercises, but carried on in the face of normal occupations and living conditions for the extent of the whole retreat. The director should determine, along with the retreatant, the amount of time each day possible for prayer and divide up the matter accordingly. If an hour and a half can be secured daily by the retreatant, the retreat could progress slowly, with almost a single point providing enough material for such a length of prayer. For example, in the First Exercise of the First Week, each single example of sin might provide the matter to be considered in prayer for that day. So, too, in the mysteries of Our Lord's life, the director may find it helpful to have the retreatant return to the same mystery for three or four days in succession.

SPIRITUAL EXERCISES

[21]. The structure of these exercises has the purpose of leading a person to a true spiritual freedom. This goal is attained by bringing one to put one's life in order in such a way that no decision or choice is made under the influence of a disordered attachment or love.

PRESUPPOSITION

[22]. For a good relationship to develop between the retreatant and the director and for the continual progress of the retreat, a mutual respect is very necessary. This may be especially true in areas of scriptural and theological presentation. A favorable interpretation by the director or by the retreatant should always be given to the other's statement. If misinterpretation seems possible, it should be cleared up with Christian understanding. So, too, if actual error seems to be held, the best possible interpretation should be presented so that a more correct understanding might develop.

THE FOUNDATION: FACT AND PRACTICE, [23]

Man was created freely out of love by God who desires to share his life forever with man, if man will freely love God in return. The whole world which has been created by God is given over to man to help him grow in his love response and so to fill this world with the order of God's love between man and man, and man and creation.

Man should readily make use of all God's gifts of creation insofar as they do help him develop more as a loving person, but where some gifts stifle such a growth in love or cause it to be lost, a man must turn away from them and let himself be free from them. As a result, in practice we must be free before all that has been created. For example, as far as we are concerned, we should hold in balance health and sickness, riches and poverty, honor and dishonor, a long life and a short life, and so on.

The only thing which moves us and the one choice which matters is the single notion of why we are created--to be able better to respond more fully in love to the love of God and to be able ever more fully to grow in that response.

Note

This consideration is to be read over by the retreatant a few times each day during the first few days of the retreat. As is evident, these words express the basic Christian catechesis in the general terms of salvation. The prayer of the retreatant at this time may well be guided by scriptural texts which will enlighten and reinforce the notions contained in this foundation (see the suggested SCRIPTURE TEXTS, A, numbers 1-13, pages 72-73 below).

A Contemporary Reading of

THE FIRST WEEK

First Exercise, [45-53]

PREPARATION: I will always take a moment to call to mind the attitude of reverence with which I approach this privileged time with God.
I ask that everything about this hour may truly be my response of
praise and service to Him.

GRACE: There is an importance in my speaking out the area of my
need for God's grace according to the time, subject matter, and my own
dispositions during the retreat. Perhaps it will also act as a preparation of my inner being for an openness to God's entrance into a
particular area of my life.

In this First Exercise, the grace I seek is the gift of feeling
shame and confusion before God as I consider the effects of even one
sin and then compare my own sinful life.

THE SETTING: (1) the angels who rebelled against God.

It has been a deep part of our Christian heritage to understand
that the first rejection of God's love in is creation is found among
his special messengers, the angels. Theologically and spiritually,
the sin of the angels exemplified the radical choice of self before
God, which is the essence of sin and the terrifying but necessary
consequence of rejecting the very source of all my life and love.
Pure spirits of decisive knowledge and totalizing love, the angels
somehow were presented with the choice which God continues to give
to each person he has lovingly made--whether he freely chooses to
respond to the life and love which He offers to him. Some angels
chose to reject his free offer of love and life with Him forever.
Immediately by closing themselves off from God, they changed from a
life of grace to a death-hatred of God and found themselves in their
own choice of hell.

I mull over this sin in my mind, letting its decisiveness strike deep into my heart, and then I look to my many rejections of God's love.

THE SETTING: (2) the sin of Adam and Eve.

In the Biblical account of how sin entered into our world from the time of the first man, we once again get a picture of a very simple but direct rejection of God's love. Adam and Eve want to be as God is, and so they are described as eating the forbidden fruit of the tree of knowledge. Both try to escape the responsibility of the choice which each one has made by trying to shift the blame to someone or something else. The effect of this one sin is not only the loss of God's special sharing of his life in grace for all mankind, but also the continuing flow of evil perpetrated by men upon their fellowmen and their world.

I consider the effect of this first sin of man for himself and for all his posterity. I let the destructiveness of evil become fully present to my attention. If one sin can wreak such havoc, what about my own sinfulness?

THE SETTING: (3) the man who goes to hell.

There is the possibility of a man making a definitive "no" as his response to God's love and ratifying that "no" even in his death. By the "no" he has given to God, he has chosen himself and therefore all the opposite of the love and life forces which can have their source only in God. He has condemned himself to the death of hell for all eternity.

How can I measure the number of "no's" which I have spoken to God up to this time? What can I say to God about myself?

COLLOQUY: I put myself before Jesus Christ our Lord, present before

me on the cross. I talk to him about how he created me out of love,
and then he became man out of love, so emptying himself as to pass
from eternal life to death here in time, even death on a cross, that
by his obedience of love given to his Father he might die for our
sins.

I look to myself and ask, just letting the question penetrate
my being:

"What have I done for Christ?"
"What am I doing for Christ?"
"What ought I to do for Christ?"

As I look upon Jesus as he hangs upon the cross, I shall ponder whatever God may bring to my attention.

Close with an Our Father.

Second Exercise, [55-61]

PREPARATION: I always come to prayer, conscious of the reverence I owe to my God.

GRACE: In this Second Exercise, I will ask God for the gift of a growing and intense sorrow, even to the depth of tears if it be his grace, for all my sins.

THE SETTING: I as a sinner before a loving God and all his gifts of creation.

Without the detail of an examination of conscience, I will let pass before my mind all my sins and sinful tendencies that permeate my life from my youth up to the very present moment. I let the weight of such evil, all stemming from me, be felt throughout my whole being.

To gain even greater perspective on my sin, I reflect that out of me, one human person among the millions of men who live, so much evil, hatred, and death can come forth. What can I compare myself to--a sewer polluting the waters of the river of life? a walking contagion of diseases who continues to walk throughout my world, affecting it and my fellowmen without warning?

I feel the weight and horror of so many effects of my sinful acts.

I put myself before God, and look at the contrast: God, the source of life, and I, a cause of death; God, the source of love, and I, with all my petty jealousies and hatreds; God, from whom all good gifts come, and I, with my attempts to win favor, buy attention, be well-thought of, and so on.

I look at my world. Everything cooperates to continue to give me life and strength. I look at the whole support system of air, warmth,

light and darkness, products of the earth, works of men's hands--
everything contributes to my well-being.

I think of the people who have prayed for me and love me. The
whole communion of saints has interest in my salvation and actively
works and prays to try to help me.

Everywhere I look, the more astonished I become, seeing so much
good coming in on me, while I issue forth so many evils.

COLLOQUY: How can I respond to a God so good to me in himself and
surrounding me with the goodness of his holy ones and all the gifts
of his creation? All I can do is give thanks, wondering at his forgiving love, which continues to give me life up to this very moment.
By his grace, I want to amend.

Close with an Our Father.

Third Exercise, [62-63]

PREPARATION: There will be the usual prayerful reverence, consciously recalled as I enter into this formal prayer period.

GRACE: As in the Second Exercise, I continue to beg Our Lord for the gift of a growing and intense sorrow, even to the depth of tears if it be his grace, for all my sins.

THE SETTING: Rather than take up new subject-matter for consideration, I should return to those thoughts and feelings which struck me forcefully from the First and Second Exercises. I will review those areas in which I felt greater consolation or desolation or, in general, greater spiritual appreciation. The idea of the repetition is to let sink further into my heart the movements of God through the means of subject matter already presented.

In the midst of these considerations, a threefold colloquy is suggested, to show the intensity of my desire for God's gift of sorrow.

COLLOQUY:

(a) First I will go to Mary, our Mother, that she may ask, on my behalf, grace for three favors from her Son and Lord:

1. A deep realization of what sin in my life is, and a feeling of abhorrence at my own sinful acts;

2. Some understanding of the disorder in my life due to sin and sinful tendencies, that I may begin to know how to amend my life and bring order into it;

3. An insight into the world that stands opposed to Christ, that I may put off from myself all that is worldly and vain.

Then I will say a Hail Mary or a Memorare, or the like.

(b) Next in the company of Mary, I will ask the same petitions of her Son that Jesus may obtain these graces from the Father for me.

Then I will say the "Soul of Christ" or some such prayer to Jesus.

(c) Finally I will approach the Father, having been presented by both Jesus and Mary. Again I will make the same requests of the Father, that He, the giver of all good gifts, may grant them to me.

Then I will close with an Our Father.

Fourth Exercise, [64]

This period of prayer is meant to be a repetition again--sometimes called a summary or a résumé. The hope is that the mind becomes less and less active with ideas since the subject matter does not change, and as a result the heart is more and more central to the way I find myself responding. The prayer period itself should probably be less active on one hand, and yet on the other by the grace of God it will grow in intensity. The intensity of the prayer should be concretized by praying once again in the manner of the threefold colloquy.

Fifth Exercise, [65-71]

PREPARATION: The usual prayerful reverence is recalled.

GRACE: I will beg for a deep sense of the pain of loss which en-
velops the damned, so that if I were ever to lose sight of the loving
goodness of God, at least the fear of such a condemnation will keep
me from falling into sin.

THE SETTING: an experience of hell.

St. Paul speaks of our being able to grasp the breadth and
length and height and depth of Christ's love and experiencing this
love which surpasses all knowledge (Eph. 3: 18-19). At its opposite
pole, I try to experience the breadth and length and height and depth
of hell--the despair of facing a cross with no one on it, the turning
out upon a world which has no God, the total emptiness of living, an
environment pervasive with hatred and self-seeking, a living death.

I bring the whole of my being into the vividness of this experience. I let all the horror of sin which has been the fruit of
my previous prayer periods wash over me in an immersing flood.
In many ways, this setting is the most passive of prayer experiences;
it is not a matter of thinking new thoughts or even of looking for
new images, but rather building on the whole experience of sin in
which I have immersed myself in the past prayer periods. It is
akin to the passive way my senses take in sights, smells, sounds,
feelings, as an automatic datum for my attention. I know that the
total felt-environment of sin, in whatever ways it can be most
vividly mine, is the setting for this period of prayer.

COLLOQUY: Once I have let the awfulness of this experience sink
deep within me, I begin to talk to Christ our Lord about it. I talk
to him about all the men who have lived--the many who lived before
his coming and who deliberately closed in upon themselves and chose

such a hell for all eternity, the many who walked with him in his own country and who rejected his call to love, the many who still keep rejecting the call to love and remain locked in their own chosen hell.

I will give thanks to Jesus that he has not put an end to my life and allowed me to fall into any of these groups. All I can do is give thanks to him that up to this very moment he has shown himself so loving and merciful to me.

Close with an Our Father.

HELPS TO PROCEEDING IN THE FIRST WEEK, [72]

The model of exercises presented here indicates the way of
proceeding in the First Week. The usual prayer pattern consists of
five formal prayer periods of one hour each. Two presentations of
matter are given--in the First and Second Exercises. The remaining
three periods of prayer are meant to be less demanding of thought,
simpler and quieter, and a deepening of what a person has been moved
by. The last or fifth period of prayer (traditionally called an
Application of Senses) is meant to be least cognitive; it is an attempt to let all that has been my experience in the previous prayer
periods to pour over me once again in one summarizing and totalizing
experience, out of which I can once again speak to my God.

A typical day of the First Week could use the Five Exercises
just as they are. Each day of the Week could continue to be a repetition of these exact same exercises. There is also the possibility of
using various scripture texts to let God's word enlighten the experience indicated in the exercises. In this way, scripture texts
may so be chosen that the experience of just the First or Second
Exercise may permeate the entire day for two or three days apiece.

In any case, the pattern of the day as well as of the Week is
meant to be clear. Each day should begin with no more than two
presentations of scriptural matter, with the succeeding repetitions
allowing the prayer to grow simpler, quieter, and more affective.
So, too, the First Week is seen as a progression from days of more
active thought and turmoil of feeling to its closing days of deep
sorrow, acceptance, and thanks to God my Savior. The First Week
suggests all that is integral to the basic Christian conversion experience: "Repent and believe the good news."

There is also the possibility of including other matter for
consideration in this First Week when it is judged that it will be
helpful for this particular retreatant. Matter on death itself or

judgment might be presented in a manner similar to the exercises indicated in the First Week or else in a scriptural way. The only norm
for the presentation of further ideas is the good progress of the
retreatant.

Although five exercises are suggested for the duration of the
First Week, age, condition of health, and the physical constitution
of the exercitant may indicate that four exercises or less may be
more profitable. When five exercises are used, the retreat day is
ordinarily patterned to begin with the first period of prayer at
midnight. Midnight does not describe actual time, but rather indicates that the prayer period should be set after an initial experience of deep sleep, which for many people comes within some two to
three hours of sleeping time. It is at this time when both body and
mind are relaxed and quiet that the prayer period can be very fruit-
ful. The other four periods of prayer can easily be spaced throughout the day.

Aids for Prayer, [73-90]

The purpose of these directions is to help one to be better
disposed as he moves into the formal prayer periods and so to be
more open to the movements of God within him.

A. Recollection

My whole day should be consistent with my prayer. There are
particular moments within the day that can be capitalized on to help
bring this about:

1. As I go to bed, I briefly recall the area about which my
prayer will center on the following day. I ask God's blessings on my
efforts this coming day.

2. When I wake up, I should not let my thoughts roam at random,
but once again I will recall the direction of this whole day's prayer
and ask for God's continual help. Insofar as I am able, I will find
it an aid to keep myself in this recollected mood all the while I dress.

3. As it has been noted in the description of the First Exercise and thereafter, a conscious recall of what I am about and whose presence I am in is most helpful at the beginning of each formal prayer period. This should be done very briefly, just to establish the sense of reverence which should pervade my prayer time.

4. In a similar way, every prayer exercise closes with what has been called a colloquy. Colloquy is a term that describes the intimate conversation between the Father and me, Christ and me, Mary or one of the saints and me, and so on. This conversation happens on the occasion of my putting myself as totally as I can into the setting of the exercise. Once I am taken into the setting of the prayer, I will find that I speak or listen as God's Spirit moves me-- sometimes as sinner, sometimes as child, at other times as lover or friend, and so on. A colloquy does not take place at any particular time within the period of prayer; it takes place as I respond within the setting of the exercise. It is true that I should mark the actual end of the hour of prayer with a definite closure--usually the Our Father or some such common prayer is a reverent way of signifying the end of this formal prayer period.

B. Position

1. Formal prayer can be made in almost any bodily position. Certain positions are more helpful for some people than for others, just as certain positions are more helpful at one time in prayer than at another. The important aspect of position is found in the criteria whether I can be at ease and yet attentive, reverent yet relaxed. And so kneeling, sitting, standing, prostrate are all potential positions for prayer. Walking, too, may lend itself to praying well if it can image the relaxation and reflectivity of the exercise. But walking often can become a restless pacing back and forth which may have its effect upon the restlessness of the prayer of the inner man.

The only restriction upon positions in prayer arises from my

awareness that a certain position may be a distraction for others,
e.g. prostrate in a church or public chapel, and thereby the position
calls attention to myself and should not be used.

2. Once I have adopted a position in prayer and my prayer is
going well, I should not readily change position because again the
outward restlessness or shifting of position can jar the inner calm
of prayer. Often a certain rhythm of kneeling and sitting, standing
or walking, is helpful according to the moods of reflection and intense begging within the exercise.

C. Review

1. After an exercise is finished, I should review what happened
during the past hour--not so much what ideas did I have, but more
the movements of consolation, desolation, fear, anxiety, boredom,
and so on, and perhaps something about my distractions, especially
if they were deep or disturbing. I may thank God for his favors and
ask pardon for my own negligences of the prayer time. Often it is
good to signalize the difference of this review of prayer from the
prayer period itself by some change of place or position.

2. I should spend about fifteen minutes in such a review. I
may find it very helpful to jot down the various reflections that
strike me so that I can more easily discuss with my director what
has been my progress from prayer period to prayer period of this
past day.

D. Environment

My whole surrounding, as well as my own deportment, can con-
tribute to the prayerful atmosphere of the retreat or detract from
it. Some areas which I could pay special attention to are:

1. During the First Week exercises, I may find it conducive
to a deeper entrance into the mystery of sin and evil by setting

my prayer periods in places which are dark and deprived of light--
keeping my own room dark, taking advantage of the dimness of a chapel
or church, and so on. In general, I should restrict my movements
during this week, avoiding the pleasantness of sun and beauties of
nature, the better to focus my attention on the darkness and loath-
someness of sin.

I should continue to adapt such directions as these to fit the
particular mood of the prayer of the Week in which I am currently
involved.

2. In regard to myself during the First Week, it is important
that I keep my attention on the matter at hand, and do not subtly
seek for ways to escape and relieve the awfulness of sin which may
be building up within me. I should not dwell on things which would
give me joy and pleasure--whether friends, occupations, music, food,
and so on. Rather I should keep my thoughts more focused on the
serious side of life.

For the same reason, I do not try to find occasions to laugh,
knowing how often laughter can be the attempt to escape the uneasiness of a situation. So, too, I must be more conscious of not trying
to look around for distractions; it is helpful to keep a certain
modesty of the eyes--always with the intention of aiding the single-
ness of focus within my whole prayer environment.

E. Penance

1. General Description

Penance must always be seen in terms of my love response to God.
Penance can be divided into two kinds: interior and exterior penance.
The more important is interior penance; it is the grace which is
sought throughout the First Week and can be described as a deep
sorrow for one's sins and a firm purpose of amendment, especially
in terms of an ever more full-hearted response of love in God's

service. Confession received its formal name of the sacrament of
penance (now called the sacrament of reconciliation) because of these
interior sentiments of the sacramental encounter.

Exterior penance properly flows out of the grace of interior
penance. It consists in taking on a certain self-inflicted punish-
ment, either through denying ourselves something or through some
positive action, to concretize our regret and resolution about our
failings in our love response to God and neighbor. There are times,
however, when exterior penance does not flow out of grace already
received, but rather I take on this kind of penance to signalize further my effort and prayer in begging God for the gift of interior
penance. In this latter case, I must be very diligent in following
the advice of my director. The reason why advice is important is
that more penance is better for some, and less for others. When I
am seeking a particular grace and I seem not to find it, it may be
the time for working out with the director some alternating periods
of days in which I practice some penance and days in which I do not.
The counsel of the director is very important at this time since I
easily can be taken in by the subtle deception of thinking I can
force God's hand by my penance or more generally that I am the one
who can bring about such a gift because of my penance. Another
reason that the director should always be kept informed lies in the
area of my own self-deception: a) either I am too ready to try to
escape from any penance by using all kinds of subterfuges, such as
"it is medieval," "I am not strong enough," "it's not for me," and
so on; b) or I am not properly ordered in my use of penance so that
I attempt too much fasting, or too many vigils, or try to take on
certain discomforts with the result that my prayer begins to suffer
or I so weaken myself in this way very gradually that I am not able
to sustain the retreat. Working with my director, I may be granted
the grace by God our Lord, who knows our nature far better than we
do, to understand what penance is suitable for me and when are the
more suitable times for doing some penance.

Ordinarily just as in the positions of prayer, I do not make
a change in doing or not doing penance if God's grace continues to be
operative in leading me ever deeper into the exercises of the retreat.
So, too, at certain times during the retreat, penance seems to be
called forth whereas at other times penance would add a jarring note
to my prayer. In every case, the counsel of the director is most
important.

2. Purpose of Exterior Penance

Three principal purposes for performing some exterior penance
at certain times are:

(a) Traditionally described, penance makes satisfaction for past
sins. Knowing that we truly are body-persons, we have the experience
of "the spirit is willing, but the flesh is weak." This is oftentimes true because of the very areas of sinfulness in our past. The
taking on of a bodily penance is an attempt to bring about that one-
ness of my inner and outer man to go specifically against the traces
and scars which sin has left in me.

(b) In a similar way, I take on exterior penance as a concrete
reminder to myself that I do have a control to exercise, especially
as I perform penances that touch those areas of my life where little
or no control has been shown in the past. By the grace of God, this
example of control through the exercise of penance shows forth the
growth of my own human freedom.

(c) More directly relevant to the retreat, perhaps, I perform
some exterior penance because of some grace or gift I desire very
earnestly and I want to involve the wholeness of my being in this
request before God. Often when such grace is granted, for example,
the gift of deep sorrow for one's sins in the First Week or the gift
of anguish with Christ in anguish in the Third Week, I may then feel
moved to do some penance to enter more fully into the mysteries about

which I am praying.

3. Kinds of Exterior Penance

Three principal ways of performing some exterior penance are:

(a) Eating: if we do away with what is superfluous, it is not penance, but temperance. We do penance when we deny ourselves something of what is proper and good for us. We should never do away with what is necessary for us since then we would be destroying the very purpose of our taking on penance--that we might better respond to God in the prayer exercises of the retreat. If any physical harm or illness results from penance in this area, we should be aware that it is not suitable penance for us.

(b) Sleep: if we do away with the superfluous in what is pampering and soft, it is not penance. We do penance when we take something away in our manner of sleeping that is proper and good for us. Once again if we find ourselves too sleepy to pray or eventual illness results, we know that we have overstepped the bounds of suitable penance. People truly differ in their sleep needs, and we should always try to get enough that will enable us to work full-heartedly in God's service.

(c) Bodily penances: there has been a tradition among many religious groups to have commonly recognized bodily penances, such as the wearing of a hairshirt, the taking of a discipline or whipping oneself with light cords, and the wearing of some kind of blunt-pointed chain around the waist or arm or leg. These kinds of penances coming down through our Christian tradition still may point the way to profitable forms of bodily penance today.

It should be obvious that bodily penances are not meant to cause wounds, sickness, and so on, but rather they are aimed at willingly sought out pain or discomfort because I am motivated by love. The possible areas of taking on discomfort or seeking out inconveniences

for penance are very numerous, and those are chosen as most suitable
and safe forms of penance which we find make us more aware of our
attempts to express our love for God and for our fellowmen.

F. The Examination of Conscience and Confession, [24-44, 90]

1. Although the retreat is already an inwardly reflective time,
it is often found helpful to set aside a brief time about midway in
the day and again at the end of the day before retiring in a formal
review of how I have spent the day. Within the retreat, this examination of conscience is not so much aimed at reviewing the areas of
sinfulness, but rather at the fulfillment of all those aids of position, recollection, environment, and so on, which are meant to inte-
grate my day, more wholly fixing it on God. Since the Weeks as well
as individual days within the Week may make very different demands
for such an integration, I will find this style of particular examination especially helpful in maintaining the proper spirit.

2. Some find that it is very useful to keep some sort of record
of this particular examination both to compare the noon and evening
periods as well as the progress from day to day within the Week.
Others may find a written record too mechanical and do not profit
from it. The better progress of the retreat is always the norm for
use or non-use of a particular method.

3. The format of the particular examination can be the same as
that style of prayer used for making a general examination of conscience, whether practiced daily or at the time of confession. There
are five points in this method of approach:

(a) giving thanks to God our Lord for all the favors he has
given;

(b) asking the help of the Spirit to enlighten me so that I
may see my sin as he sees it;

(c) going back over the events of the day or of the time since

29

my last confession to see the sinful acts, whether in thoughts, words, or deeds, whether of omission or commission, and the tendencies or roots of such sinful behavior;

(d) expressing my sorrow and asking God's forgiving love to heal me;

(e) praying for the strength of God's grace to help me amend my life.

4. There usually develops a desire for the sacrament of penance as one enters deeply into the exercises of the First Week. Not only should confession be encouraged, but it is well to consider the advantages of a general confession at this time:

(a) While there is no obligation to make a general confession, at a time when one has let the full burden of his sinfulness weigh him down, he comes with even greater sorrow to present to the Lord all the sin and perversities which are so deeply a part of his person.

(b) Through means of prayer, one arrives at a far deeper insight into his sins and their malice. Because the grace of the retreat has led him to this deeper knowledge and sorrow, he comes with greater fervor and openness to the healing power of Christ in the sacrament of penance.

(c) It is good to make such a confession, whether it be a general confession or not, somewhere towards the end of the First Week so that I approach the sacrament not in haste or turmoil over the recognition of my sins, but rather in accepting myself as sinner, as one always in need of radical healing, and as one who acknowledges that God alone is my Savior.

CHRIST THE KING AND HIS CALL, [91-98]

PREPARATION: I take the usual time to place myself before God in reverence.

GRACE: I will ask of Our Lord that I be able to hear his call, and that I might be ready and willing to do what he wants.

THE SETTING: There are two unequal parts in this consideration, the first one naturally leading to the more important second part.

1. In the first part, let me put myself into a mythical situation--the kind of story-truth of which fairy tales are made. I imagine a human leader, selected and raised up by God our Lord himself; every man, woman, and child of good will is drawn to listen to such a leader and is inspired to follow his call.

His address to all men rings out in words like these: "I want to overcome all diseases, all poverty, all ignorance, all oppression and slavery--in short, all the enemies of mankind. Whoever wishes to join me in this undertaking must be content with the same food, drink, clothing, and so on, as mine. So, too, he must work with me by day, and watch with me by night, and so on, that as he has had a share in the toil with me, afterwards, he may share in the victory with me."

If a leader so attractive and inspiring and so much a man of God makes such a call, what kind of a person could refuse such an invitation? How could anyone not want to be a part of so challenging and noble an adventure?

2. In the second part, I consider Jesus Christ our Lord and his call. If a human leader can have such an appeal to us, how much greater is the attraction of the God-Man, Jesus Christ, our Leader and King! His call goes out to the whole of mankind, yet he specially

calls each man in a particular way. He makes the appeal: "It is my
will to win over the whole world, to conquer sin, hatred, and death--
all the enemies between men and God. Whoever wishes to join me in
this mission must be willing to labor with me, so that by following
me in suffering, he may follow me in glory."

With God inviting and with victory assured, how can anyone of
right mind not give himself over to Jesus and his work?

Persons who are of great heart and are set on fire with zeal to
follow Jesus Christ, eternal King and Lord of all, will not only offer
themselves entirely for such a mission, but will act against anything
that would make their response less total. They would want to express themselves in some such words as these:

Eternal Lord and King of the Universe, [98]

"Eternal Lord and King of the Universe, I humbly come before
you and, supported by your mother Mary and all your saints, I offer
myself by the help of your grace to you and to your work. I profess
that it is my earnest desire and my deliberate choice, provided only
it is for your greater service and praise, to imitate you in bearing
all wrongs and all abuse and all poverty, both actual and spiritual--
if you, my Lord and King, would want to choose and admit me to such
a state and way of life."

SUGGESTED DIRECTIONS, [99-100]

1. The above exercise should be considered in formal prayer
twice during the day. The rest of the day should be free of set
prayer periods.

2. During the Second Week and thereafter, it can be profitable
to read some classic spiritual works or some biographies of holy men
and women. Scripture, too, can sometimes be used, although it is not
wise to read the Gospels since certain mysteries of our Lord's life

and ministry may call forth responses from me that are not consonant with where I am in my formal prayer periods of the retreat. The director and the retreatant should work out this area of reading together so that no influences contrary to the movement of the retreat are unwittingly introduced through the reading material.

A Contemporary Reading of

The First Day and First Contemplation
The Incarnation, [101-109]

PREPARATION: I take the usual time to place myself before God in
reverence.

GRACE: I will ask for the grace to know Jesus intimately, to love
him more intensely, and so to follow him more closely.

Preliminary Note: The following description is an attempt to point
out some of the ways of entering into the style of prayer called
contemplation. The description in words can make it sound very
mechanical. To remember that the act of praying is our single focus
will pour life-blood into the dead body of words.

THE SETTING: I try to enter into the vision of God, in his triune
life, looking upon our world: men aimless, men despairing, men hate-
ful and killing, men sick and dying, the old and the young, the rich
and the poor, the happy and the sad, some being born and some being
laid to rest. The leap of divine joy: God knows that the time has
come when the mystery of his salvific plan, hidden from the beginning
of the world, will become manifest.

    This is the context of the Annunciation scene, which we find in
the text of Scripture (Luke 1:26-38). I try to stay with the eyes of
God, and look upon the young girl Mary, as she is greeted by Gabriel.

    I let myself be totally present to the scene, hearing the nuances
of the questions, seeing the expression in the face and eyes, watching
the gestures and movements which tell us so much about a person.

    I notice how our triune God works--so simply and so quietly. A
world goes on, apparently oblivious of the total revolution which

has begun. I look at Mary's complete way of responding to her Lord and God.

COLLOQUY: As I find myself immersed in the setting of this mystery of the Incarnation, I may want just to stay with Mary or with our Lord, who has now become man for me. Sometimes I may want to speak out my joy, my thanks, my wonder, or my praise. According to the light I have received, I will beg for the grace to know and to be able to draw close to Jesus, my Lord. I will close the prayer period with an Our Father.

The Second Contemplation
The Nativity, [110-117]

PREPARATION: the usual preparatory reverence.

GRACE: I will continue to ask for the grace to know Jesus intimately, to be able to love him more intensely, and so to follow him more closely.

THE SETTING: The familiar story of the Nativity should allow me the more easily to be present fully to the persons and places of this mystery. Whatever methods will help me enter into the whole scene and to be with the persons involved I should embrace.

To be able to enter into the deep-down stillness of this night, to be able to see this very human baby with all the wonder which comes from eyes of faith, to watch how Mary and Joseph handle them-selves, their own response to God at this time--these are various aspects or focuses of the mystery which I may find myself drawn to.

I should take note of the hardship which is already so much a part of Jesus' presence in our world. The labors of the journey to Bethlehem, the struggles of finding a shelter, the poverty, hunger, thirst, heat, and cold, the insults which meet the arrival of

A Contemporary Reading of

God-with-us--all this that He might die on the cross for me.

COLLOQUY: According to the different aspects which I may focus upon
at any one time within the prayer period, I should respond accordingly,
for example, to Mary, Joseph, Jesus, the Father. Perhaps there will
be little to say because this style of contemplation is often more
a "being with" experience than a word-response.

I will always bring the period of prayer to a close with an Our
Father.

The Third Contemplation
A Repetition, [118-119]

This period will be a repetition of the First and Second Exercises. After the preparatory reverence and the petition for the
usual grace, the matter from the First and/or Second Exercises will
be used. Quite often one will find that he would like to return to
a particular mystery in itself, such as the Incarnation; or one might
find that in this Third Contemplation, the original first two settings
flow one into the other. In making such a repetition, it is always
important to return to those parts or points of focus where one has
experienced understanding, consolation, or desolation.

Since the entrance into the setting of such a repetition is
frequently very simple, the emphasis more and more is fixed on my
personal response which is represented by the colloquy. I should
always remember to close the prayer period with an Our Father.

In this repetition and in all those which follow, the usual manner of proceeding should be observed as it was explained in the First
Week. The subject matter is changed, but the same manner of repeat-
ing the exercise is continued.

The Fourth Contemplation
A Résumé, [120]

This period will reinforce the notion of the repetition as outlined in the preceding paragraph. Note usually how the prayer grows
simpler in the matter considered, allowing always for a deeper and
deeper personal response to the mysteries of Christ's life.

The Fifth Contemplation
Application of Senses, [121-126]

Traditionally this prayer period has been described as an application of the five senses to the matter of the day.

After the preparatory prayer and the petition for the usual
grace, this last period of prayer within my day is meant to be my
own "letting go," a total immersion of myself into the mystery of
Christ's life this day. Just as when we tried to enter into the experience of hell within the First Week, so here too, it is not a
matter of thinking new thoughts or of trying new methods of getting
into the mystery. Rather the notion is to build upon all the experiences which have been a part of my prayer day. Again it is akin
to the passive way my senses take in sights, smells, sounds, feelings,
as an automatic datum for my attention. The total felt-environment
of the particular mystery of Christ's life, in whatever ways it can
be most vividly mine, is the setting for this final period of prayer
in each day.

COLLOQUY: I respond as I am so moved by God's grace. I close with
an Our Father.

FURTHER DIRECTIONS, [127-131]

1. It is important to point out that throughout this Week and
the subsequent Weeks, I should read only the mystery which is the
subject matter of my contemplation. I should not read any mystery

which is not to be used on that particular day or at that hour, so that the contemplation of one mystery does not interfere with another.

2. An ideal suggested order of the prayer day is: the First Exercise on the Incarnation should take place at midnight (i.e., after an initial period of sleep), the second in early morning, the third in later morning, the fourth in the afternoon, and the fifth in the evening.

The order of the prayer day has its importance in terms of the whole ordering process of one's life, which is the end of the Ex-ercises.

3. The Second Week may well call for some adaptation in the number of prayer periods. Whether the person is old or young, weak or strong, quite often the First Week has been a tiring experience. For that reason, it is often better not to use the midnight medita-tion time, with the possibility of either five or four periods of prayer spread out throughout the day.

4. It is probably obvious that some adaptations should be made in terms of the aids for prayer.

Specifically, as soon as I awake, I should recall the direction of this whole day's prayer, with the desire to grow in my intimate knowledge of Jesus Christ in order to love and serve him better.

Another help will be to recall at various times in the day the mysteries of the life of Christ our Lord from his Incarnation up to the mystery I am currently contemplating.

So, too, I as a retreatant should use darkness and light, the chapel or the outdoors, insofar as I understand that it fits well with the mystery I am contemplating.

In regard to penance, again I should conduct myself according to the mysteries under consideration. Some may call for penance, others will not.

As a general reminder, I should continue to observe very carefully all the aids for prayer for the good progress of the retreat.

5. In a way of preparing myself similar to the preparation for the first prayer period of the day, I should come to all periods of prayer in the following manner: as soon as I note that it is time for the next prayer period, even before moving on, I will bring to mind where I am going, before whom I am to appear, and briefly recall the subject matter of the exercise. Then with a certain anticipation of God's gifts, I shall proceed to the usual preparatory reverence, as I enter into the very exercise itself.

The Second Day, [132]

On the second day, for the first and second contemplations, the Presentation in the Temple (see no. 35 below on page 76), and the Flight into Exile in Egypt (see no. 36 below), should be used. Two repetitions, along with or including the Application of the Senses, should be done as on the First Day.

Note: As was stated previously, sometimes it will be profitable, no matter how strong and well-disposed the retreatant, to make some changes in the first part of this Second Week, in order to attain better what is desired. So the first contemplation would be the one on rising in the morning. Then there would be one later in the morning, with another in the afternoon, and the final one in the evening.

The Third Day, [134]

On the third day, use the contemplations on the Obedience of the Child Jesus to his parents (see no. 38 below), and the Finding of the Child Jesus in the Temple (see no. 39 below). As usual there will follow the two repetitions, along with or including the Application of the Senses.

INTRODUCTION TO THE CONSIDERATION
OF
DIFFERENT STATES OF LIFE, [135]

One way of considering the mysteries of Jesus' early life is to
see the interpretative direction in which they point. The ordinary
life of the Christian is exemplified in Christ's obedience to his
parents in the ordinary life of Nazareth. But the call to service
in the Father's house is already manifested in the mystery of Jesus'
remaining in the temple at the age of twelve to the consternation of
his mother and father.

While I continue to contemplate his life, let me begin to examine
myself and ask to what state of life or to what kind of life style is
God in his loving providence leading me.

As a kind of introduction to this, in the next exercise, I will
consider the way Christ our Lord draws men, and on the other hand,
the way the enemy of our human nature enslaves. At the same time I
may also begin to see how I should prepare myself to a continued
growth in whatever state or kind of life God our Lord may be moving
me to choose.

The Fourth Day

A Meditation:
TWO LEADERS, TWO STRATEGIES, [136-147]

We will consider Christ, our Leader and Lord, our God and
Brother, and we will consider Satan, the personal enemy who
sums up all the evils that beset mankind.

PREPARATION: the usual preparatory reverence.

GRACE: Here it will be to ask for the gift of being able to recognize the deceits of Satan and help to guard myself against them; and
also it will be to ask for a knowledge of the true life exemplified
in Jesus Christ, my Lord and my God, and the grace to live my life
in His way.

THE SETTING: There are two unequal parts in this consideration, the
first one shedding light upon and giving direction to the more important second part.

1. To sum up all the forces of evil in the person of Satan
makes us face the enormous power and oppression of evil itself.
Keeping true to our own experience of the world, let us reflect how
evil pummels the relations between nations and between peoples within
a single country, so that no nation, no city, no state of life, no
individual is left unscathed. I try to grasp the strategy of Satan as
he attempts ever to enslave men and the world according to his design.
Men will find themselves tempted to covet riches, so that because
they possess some thing(s) they find themselves seeking and accepting
the honor and esteem of this world. From such honor arises the false
sense of identity and value in which false pride has its roots.

So the strategy is simple: riches (or "this is mine") to honor
(or "look at me") to pride (or "I AM . . ."). By these three steps,

41

the evil one leads men to all other vices.

2. Now let us look at Jesus Christ, who calls himself "the way,
the truth, and the life." Notice how gently, but insistently, Jesus
continues to call followers of all kinds and sends them forth to
spread his good news to all men, no matter what their state or condition. Jesus adopts a strategy which is just the opposite of Satan:
try to help men, not enslave or oppress them. His method: attract
men to the highest spiritual poverty, and should it please God, and
should he draw them to want to choose it, even to a life of actual
poverty. Being poor, they will be led to accept and even to desire
the insults and contempt of the world. The result will be a life of
true humility.

Jesus' strategy is simple too: if I have been graced with the
gift of poverty, then I am rich; if I have nothing, I have no power
and I am despised and receive the contempt of the world; having
nothing, my only possession is Christ and this is to be really true
to oneself--the humility of man whose whole reality lies in being
created and redeemed in Christ.

Through these three steps, Jesus and his apostles lead men to
all other virtues.

COLLOQUY: Because of the importance of coming to some understanding
of the opposing forces of these two leaders and their strategies, I
will enter into the intensity of the prayer by addressing and begging
favors from Mary, Christ, and the Father.

(a) First I approach Our Lady, asking her to obtain for me
from her Son the grace-gift to be his apostle--following him in the
highest spiritual poverty, and should God be pleased thereby and want
to choose and accept me, even in actual poverty. Even greater is the
gift I seek in being able to bear the insults and the contempt of my
world, so imitating Christ my Lord ever more closely, provided only

I can suffer these without sin on the part of another and without any offense to God. Then I will say a Hail Mary or a Memorare.

(b) Next in the company of Mary, I will ask the same petitions of her Son that Jesus may obtain these same favors or gifts from the Father. Then I will say the "Soul of Christ" or some such prayer to Jesus.

(c) Finally I will approach the Father, having been presented by both Jesus and Mary. Again, I will make the same requests of the Father that he, the giver of all good gifts, may grant such favors to me. Then I will close with an Our Father.

Note, [148]

This exercise should be made three or four times within a single day. The same three colloquies, with Our Lady, with her Son, and with the Father, will close all the exercises as well as the one on the Three Types of Persons, which follows as the last (either fourth or fifth) prayer period of the day.

A Contemporary Reading of

THREE TYPES OF PERSONS, [149-156]

This is a meditation for the same fourth day to aid me in
my freedom of choice according to God's call to me.

PREPARATION: the usual preparatory reverence.

GRACE: I will ask that I might be free enough to choose whatever
the lead of God's grace may indicate as His particular call to me.

THE SETTING: This prayer period is devoted to a consideration of
three types of persons. Each one of them has taken in quite a few
possessions--not always with the best of motives, but in fact sometimes quite selfishly. In general, each one is a good person, and
he would like to serve God, even to the extent that if these possessions were to come in the way of his salvation, he would like to
be free of them.

(1) the First Type--"a lot of talk, but no action"

This person keeps saying that he would like to stop being so
dependent on all the things which he possesses and which seem to get
in the way of his giving his life unreservedly to God. He talks about
the importance of saving his soul, but when death comes, he is too
busy about his possessions to have taken any steps towards serving
God.

(2) the Second Type--"to do everything but the one thing necessary"

This person would like to be free of all attachments which get
in the way of his relationship with God. But he would rather work
harder or fast or pray more--really just do about anything but face
the problem which he feels holds him back in his relationship with
God. He acts as if he is negotiating with God, trying to buy God off.
So though he may do many good things, he keeps running from the

better and more honest way to face the issue.

(3) the Third Type--"to do Your will is my desire"

This person would like to be rid of any attachment which gets in the way of God's call to further life. His whole effort is to be in balance, ready to move in any direction that the call from God may take him. Whatever seems better for the service and praise of God our Lord is his whole desire and choice. Meanwhile, he strives to act in such a way that he seemingly is free of any attachments. He makes efforts neither to want to retain his possessions nor to want to give them away, unless the service and praise of God our Lord is the God-given motivation for his action. As a result, the graced desire to be better able to serve God our Lord is the cause of his accepting or letting go of anything.

COLLOQUY: I will make use of the same three colloquies described in the preceding meditation on the Two Leaders, Two Strategies.

Note, [157]

We may find it helpful at this time of the retreat when we might discover some attachment opposed to actual poverty or a repugnance to it, or when we are not indifferent to poverty and riches, to come to Jesus our Lord in prayer and beg Him to choose us to serve Him in actual poverty. We should beg with a certain insistence, and we should plead for it--but always wanting what God wants for us.

The Fifth Day, [158]

The contemplation on Our Lord's Baptism by John in the Jordan (see no. 40 below).

FURTHER DIRECTIONS, [159-160]

1. Beginning with the Fifth Day, it is suggested that only one

Scripture passage provide the prayer material for the entire day. Since the Exercises have as a primary aim the choice of a state or way of life, the purpose in limiting the amount of new material to be considered in prayer is to keep the head less occupied with many thoughts. Within the free time of these days, retreatants may likely be doing a lot of weighing of alternatives, trying to understand the lead of God in their lives. As a result, the director is encouraged to keep the prayer material itself simple and less demanding of a lot of reasoning.

Yet it should be pointed out that the number of prayer periods should be maintained, with the usual repetitions leading to the more simple gaze of the Application of the Senses for the same mystery of Christ's life.

It might also be good to recall that even though we speak of a simplifying of the prayer at this time of the retreat, we should still be most careful to observe the preparatory reverence, the petition for a specified grace, and the intimate conversation of the colloquy. Because of the intensity of the search for God's will and our response at this period of the retreat, the triple colloquy addressed to Mary, Christ, and the Father might well remain an ordinary part of these prayer periods.

2. The Particular Examen of Conscience usually made at mid-day and before retiring should continue its focus on the faults and negligences with regard to the exercises of the day, especially in view of the helps or aids to prayers which have been suggested.

The Sixth Day, [161]

The contemplation on Christ our Lord's being led into the desert to be tempted (see no. 41 below, on page 76).

The Seventh Day

The contemplation on Jesus' calls to the apostles (see no. 42 below).

The Eighth Day

The contemplation on the Eight Beatitudes (see no. 45 below).

The Ninth Day

The contemplation on Christ's walking on the water (see no. 47 below).

The Tenth Day

The contemplation on Jesus preaching in the temple (see no. 55 below).

The Eleventh Day

The contemplation on Jesus' raising of Lazarus (see no. 52 below).

The Twelfth Day

The contemplation on the triumphal entry into Jerusalem (see no. 54 below).

FURTHER DIRECTIONS, [162-164]

1. The Second Week, similar to the First, has no set number of days. According to the progress of the retreatant, especially in view of a choice which he is trying to clarify, the director may find that he might want to lengthen or shorten the Week.

In lengthening the Week, the director might suggest other

mysteries from the Gospel infancy narratives, such as the Visitation of Mary to Elizabeth, the Shepherds at Bethlehem, the Circumcision of the Child Jesus, and the Three Wise Men's Journey and Adoration. By contrast, if the director thinks it well that the Week should be shortened, he may omit some of the mysteries that have been proposed. However many mysteries are taken up in the Second Week, they only serve to introduce the retreatant into a way of prayer which will continue to enter him more deeply into the life of Christ our Lord.

2. If a retreatant is trying to clarify a choice of a state or way of life, the time for this consideration begins with the Fifth Day, where the contemplation of Our Lord's own setting forth to the Jordan determines the vocation of his own public life.

3. Before a retreatant enters into his considerations about the choice of a state or way of life, it will be very useful to spend some time mulling over the following description of Three Kinds of Humility. These should be thought over from time to time outside of the formal prayer periods from the Fifth Day onwards. Perhaps after a day or two of consideration, a retreatant may find that he does want to be gifted in the way most expressive of his love and dedication to Jesus Christ, his Lord and God. Then he should make use of the three-fold colloquy to manifest the intensity of his desire for this grace.

THREE KINDS OF HUMILITY, [165-167]

Humility lies in the acceptance of Jesus Christ as the fullness
of what it means to be human. To be humble is to live as close to
the truth as possible: that I am created to the likeness of Christ,
that I am meant to live according to the pattern of his paschal mystery, and that my whole fulfillment is found in being as near to
Christ as he draws me to himself. The following descriptions try to
sum up three different general areas on the spectrum of humility as
it is actually lived by men.

(1) The First Kind of Humility. This is living out the truth
which is necessary for salvation, and so it describes one ex-
treme of the spectrum. I would want to do nothing that would cut me
off from God--not even were I made lord of all creation or even just
to save my own life here on earth. I know that grave sin in this
sense is to miss the whole meaning of being man--one who is created
and redeemed and is destined to live forever in love with God his
Creator and Lord.

(2) The Second Kind of Humility. This kind is more perfect
than the first, and so we find ourselves somewhere along the middle
of the spectrum. My life is firmly grounded in the fact that the
reality of being man is seen fully in Jesus Christ. Just as "I have
come to do your will, O God" is the motivating force of his life, so
the only real principle of choice in my life is to seek out and do
the will of my Father. With this habitual attitude, I find that I
can maintain a certain balance in my inclinations to have riches
rather than poverty, honor rather than dishonor, or to desire a long
life rather than a short life. I would not want to turn away from
God even in small ways, because my whole desire is to respond ever
more faithfully to his call.

(3) The Third Kind of Humility. This is closer to the other
end of the spectrum, since it demands the understanding and action

of a greater grace-gift. It consists in this. I so much want the
truth of Christ's life to be fully the truth of my own that I find
myself, moved by grace, with a love and desire for poverty in order
to be with the poor Christ; a love and desire for insults in order
to be closer to Christ in his own rejection by men; a love and desire
to be considered worthless and a fool for Christ, rather than to be
esteemed as wise and prudent according to the standards of the world.
By grace, I find myself so moved to follow Jesus Christ in the most
intimate union possible, that his experiences are reflected in my
own. In that, I find my delight.

Note, [168]

If after some time for consideration a retreatant wants to move
more in the direction of this third kind of humility, it will help
much to make use of the threefold colloquy, as it has been explained
above. He should beg Our Lord to choose him for the gift of this
third kind of humility in order that he may find his own life more
patterned according to Jesus, his God and Lord--always, of course,
if this is to be for the greater praise and service of God.

INTRODUCTION TO MAKING A CHOICE
OF A STATE OR WAY OF LIFE [169]

In making a choice or in coming to a decision, only one thing
is really important--to seek and find what God calls me to at this
time of my life. I know that his call remains faithful; he has
created me for himself and my salvation is found in that love. All
my choices, then, must be consistent with this given direction of my
life.

It becomes obvious how easy it is for me to forget such a simple
truth as the end and goal of my whole existence, when I consider the
manner in which choices are often made. Many people, for example,
choose marriage, which is a means, and only secondarily consider the
service of God our Lord in marriage, though to do the will of God is
man's end. Many people first choose to make a lot of money or be
successful, and only afterwards to be able to serve God by it. And
so too in their striving for power, popularity, and so on. All of
these people exhibit an attitude of putting God into second place,
and they want God to come into their lives only after their own disordered attachment. In other words, they mix up the order of an end
and a means to that end. What they ought to seek first and above all
else, they often put last.

It is good, then, for me to recall that my whole aim in life
should be to seek to serve God in whatever way his call may come to
me. Keeping clearly before me my desire to serve God our Lord, I
can begin to search out the means of marrying or not marrying, a life
of business involvement or a life of simple frugality, and the like,
for these are all means to accomplishing the end. I will choose to
use or not use such means only through the inspiration and movement
of God's grace leading me on in his service and to my own salvation.

A Contemporary Reading of

MATTERS ABOUT WHICH A CHOICE
SHOULD BE MADE, [170-173]

The purpose of these observations is to provide a certain basic information on the matters about which decisions are very important. It contains four points and a note.

(1) When we are making a decision or choice, we are not deliberating about choices which involve sin, but rather we are considering alternatives which are lawful and good within our Catholic Church and not bad or opposed to her.

(2) There are choices which represent permanent commitment such as marriage, priesthood, and religious life. There are other choices which can be changed, such as a seeking after a successful career in business or medicine, or a decision to live according to a certain life-style.

(3) With regard to permanent commitment, our basic attitude should be that the only choice still called for is the more full-hearted gift of self to this state of life. Only this is to be noted. If it becomes apparent that the choice or decision has not been made as it should have been and if there has been a certain disordered attachment involved, our first response is one of sorrow and an attempt to amend by putting our efforts into righting the situation. Professional help or the help of friends who can be objective, along with legitimate authority itself, must oftentimes play an important role at this time of reevaluation.

There is no sense trying to say God's call is directly involved in a choice which we have made because of a disordered attachment. For the call from God is not at the whim of faulty information, sensual emotion, or disordered love.

(4) When we are dealing with matters which can be changed,

there is no reason to feel anxiety or to move to an unhealthy intro-
spection if we seem to have come to the decision properly and in good
order when we first made it. Our one desire should be to find my
continued growth in the way of life I have chosen.

Note, [174]

If we have poorly come to a decision in matters that are changeable, we should try to make a choice in the proper way whether it
would be maintaining the same pattern of life or it would demand a
change. For our desire is to praise and serve God in all our choices
so that he can continue to work through us for the good of our fellowmen and our world.

THREE TIMES WHEN A CORRECT AND GOOD CHOICE
OF A STATE OR WAY OF LIFE
MAY BE MADE, [175-187]

(1) First Time. There is a time of clarity which comes with
undeviating persistence. We think of the dramatic change in St. Paul
on the road to Damascus, for once he began to respond to the Jesus
whom he had been persecuting he never hesitated. From the brief
description of Matthew's call in the Gospel, we could draw a similar
example. We can feel very gifted when God's call is so unmistakably
focused in its drawing power, for this is the best of times for decisions.

(2) Second Time. Quite frequently we experience a time of alternating certainties and doubts, of exhilarating strength and de-
bilitating weakness, of consolation and of desolation. As a matter
of fact, this time is very privileged, for the discernment of spirits
which is called for is an entrance into understanding a language of
God spoken within our very being. We can gain much light and understanding from the experience of consolation and desolation, and so
this time, too, is very special for correct decision-making.

(3) Third Time. Sometimes, through no fault of our own, nothing seems to be going on. We are placid, having neither the peace
of God's consolation nor the desolation of feeling his absence. It
is at this time that we can think clearly enough and since we can
distinguish no movement from God, we would describe this time as one
of our own reasoning process.

We should recall our earlier consideration about ends and means,
and so the approach is always within the context of a choice leading
to a greater service of God and so for our own salvation. The free
and peaceful use of our reasoning abilities shows forth the calm
logic of this time.

If a choice is not made within circumstances as described in the First or Second Times, then some helpful hints at proceeding during the time of calm rationality are given according to two patterns as follows:

A. First Pattern of Making a Good and Correct Choice:

(1) clearly place before my mind what it is I want to decide about;

(2) try to be like a balance at equilibrium, without leaning to either side. My end is always clearly before me, but I want to be as free towards the object of my choice as I possibly can be;

(3) pray that God our Lord enlighten and move me in the way leading to his praise and glory. Then I should use my understanding to weigh the matter carefully and attempt to come to a decision consonant with my living out God's will in my life;

(4) list and weigh the advantages and the disadvantages of the various sides of my proposed decision;

(5) consider now which alternative seems more reasonable. Then I will decide according to the more weighty motives and not from any selfish or sensual inclination;

(6) having come to the decision, I now turn to God again and ask him to accept and confirm it if it is for his greater service and glory by bringing it into the ambit of the Second or First Time.

B. Second Pattern of Making a Correct and Good Choice:

(1) Since the love of God should motivate my life, I should check myself whether the greater or less attachment for the object of choice is solely because of my Creator and Lord.

(2) I present myself with a person whom I have never met before, but who has sought my help in his attempt to respond better to God's call to him. I see what I would tell him, and then I observe the advice which I would so readily give to another for whom I want the best.

(3) If I were at the moment of death and so I would have the freedom and clarity of that time, what would be the decision I would want to have made now? I will guide myself by this insight and make my present decision in conformity with it.

(4) If I see myself standing before Christ my Judge when this life has ended, and I find myself speaking out the decision which I have made at this moment in my life. I choose now the course of action which I feel will give me happiness and joy in presenting it to Christ on the day of judgment.

Note, [188]

Even after proceeding according to the circumstances outlined above, I will take the decision which I have reached by these approaches and beg God our Lord to accept and confirm it if it is for his greater service and glory by bringing it into the ambit of the Second or First Time.

SOME DIRECTIONS FOR THE RENEWAL OF
OR RECOMMITMENT TO A STATE
OR WAY OF LIFE ALREADY CHOSEN, [189]

Often in retreat I find myself not so much faced with the
question of a new decision, but rather with the living out of a
choice already made. This can be as true of the permanent state of
life represented in marriage or priesthood as of the more changeable
way of life represented in particular jobs or positions.

During the course of the Exercises, it may be quite profitable
to take stock of how my living out of a particular means which I
have chosen is truly responding to the faithful call of God. The
service and love of God and neighbor should shine out in my dedication. At this time, I should deepen the attitudes and search out
the ways which will better enable me to live the Christ-life in my
own surroundings and environment. For my progress in living out my
life in Christ will be in proportion to the surrender of my own self-
love and of my own will and interests.

A Contemporary Reading of

THE THIRD WEEK

The First Day and First Contemplation:
The Last Supper, [190-198

PREPARATION: the usual preparatory reverence.

GRACE: The gift I seek from God is his allowing me to enter into a sorrow and shame as I stay with Christ in his sufferings borne on my behalf and because of my sins.

THE SETTING: To enter as fully as I can into the preparations for the Passover Meal and into the whole event we call the Last Supper is my purpose in this contemplation. It goes beyond picturing the scene or reading the account in words. I try to listen to the way words are spoken, I attempt to see the expression on the face, I am present with as heightened an awareness as I can muster, so that I enter into the mystery I am contemplating. The Gospel accounts depict the preparations, the Supper itself, Christ's washing of the feet of his Apostles, his giving of his Body and Blood in the Eucharist, and his final words to them.

In addition, during this Third Week, I should make even greater effort to labor with Christ through all his anguish, his struggle, his suffering, or what he desires to suffer. At the time of the Passion, I should pay special attention to how the divinity hides itself so that Jesus seems so utterly human and helpless. To realize that Christ loves me so much that he willingly suffers everything for my rejections and sins makes me question my own response--what can I do in return?

COLLOQUY: I speak out to Jesus, my Lord and Savior, and stay with him through everything that happens. Close the period with an Our Father.

Note, [199]

Because of the intimacy involved during the contemplations of

58

the Passion, it might be well to review some aspects of the time
called colloquy. Just as in human situations of taking care of the
sick or of ministering to the dying, our presence is often more important than our faltering words or awkward actions, so too to be with
Christ in his Passion describes my prayer response at this time better
than any words or actions. Previously we described the colloquy as
the intimate conversation between friends. Now we open out that description to include the depth of feeling, love, and compassion,
which allows us just to be there.

Sometimes, still, we may want to pour out our consolations, our
temptations, our fears, our hardness of heart to Christ our Lord. In
times of great need, we may find the intensity of begging reflected
in our use of the threefold colloquy. We should remember that faced
with the suffering of the Passion we may have to pray even for the
gift of letting ourselves want to experience it with Christ, according to the manner suggested after the Meditation on the Three Types
of Persons.

The Second Contemplation
The Agony in the Garden, [200-203]

PREPARATION: the usual preparatory reverence.

GRACE: I will continue to pray for the gift of being able to feel
sorrow with Christ in sorrow, to be anguished with Christ's anguish,
and even to experience tears and deep grief because of all the af-
flictions which Christ endures for me.

THE SETTING: The Gospels give the details of the event: Christ and
his disciples leaving the Upper Room to go towards the garden of
Gethsemani. There Jesus takes Peter, James, and John, and goes
apart to pray, even to experiencing such turmoil of spirit that his
sweat became as drops of blood. Waking his sleepy disciples, he
faces the mob, is identified by the kiss of Judas, and is led away

to the house of Annas. I will labor to enter as fully into the account at hand as I possibly can.

FURTHER DIRECTIONS, [204-207]

1. The second contemplation, as well as all that follow, is
done after the manner of the first contemplation dealing with the
Last Supper. During the Third Week, two Scripture passages are given
for each day, so that the usual repetitions are made, leading to the
Application of the Senses as the final period of prayer.

2. Depending upon the age, health, and condition of the retreatant, five exercises a day are encouraged, but less may be more
desirable because of particular circumstances.

3. In the Third Week, some modifications must again be made in
the helps for prayer.

Because of the subject matter of the Passion, I will make an
effort while rising and dressing to be sad and solemn because of the
great sorrow and suffering of Christ our Lord.

Throughout the day, I will be careful not to bring up pleasing
thoughts, even though they are good and holy, as for example thoughts
about the Resurrection and life of glory. Rather I will try to maintain a certain attitude of sorrow and anguish by calling to mind
frequently the labors, fatigue, and suffering which Christ our Lord
endured from the time of his birth down to the particular mystery of
the Passion which I am presently contemplating.

In a similar way, the Particular Examen of Conscience should be
applied to the exercises and my observation of the helps applicable
to this Week, just as it was done in the past Weeks.

The Second Day, [208]

1. The contemplation on events from the Garden to the house of Annas (see Scripture Texts, no. 58, on page 78 below).

2. The contemplation on events from the house of Annas to the house of Caiphas (see no. 59, on page 78).
The usual repetitions should be made, with the Application of the Senses being the final prayer period of the day.

The Third Day

1. The contemplation on events from the house of Caiphas to the house of Pilate (see no. 60, on page 78).

2. The contemplation on events from the house of Pilate to the palace of Herod (see no. 61).
Then the repetitions and Application of the Senses as noted above.

The Fourth Day

1. The contemplation on events from Herod's palace back to the house of Pilate (see no. 62).

2. The contemplation on events with Pilate (see no. 62).
The same procedure should be followed for the repetitions.

The Fifth Day

1. The contemplation on events from the house of Pilate to the crucifixion (see no. 63).

2. The contemplation on events from the raising of the Cross to Jesus' death (see no. 64).
The repetitions follow as usual.

A Contemporary Reading of

The Sixth Day

1.   The contemplation on events from the taking down from the Cross to the burial (see no. 65).

2.   The contemplation on events from the burial to Mary's waiting in sorrow.
The repetitions follow as usual.

The Seventh Day

1.   The contemplation on events of the whole Passion.

2.   A repetition on the whole of the Passion.
For the rest of the day, let the effect of Christ's death permeate my world. Consider the desolation of Our Lady, her great sorrow and weariness, and also that of the disciples.

Note, [209]

If we want to spend more time on the Passion, the mysteries can be so divided that, for example, only the Supper is considered in one prayer period, then Christ's washing of the feet of his Apostles in another, next the institution of the Eucharist, and finally the farewell discourse of Christ. The other mysteries which make up the total Passion account could be similarly divided up.

After the Passion has been contemplated in its various mysteries over some days, there is the possibility of taking one full day on the first half of the Passion, and a second day on the other half, and a final day reviewing the whole of the Passion.

But if we wish to spend less time on the Passion, we could use a different mystery for each of the prayer periods, eliminating all repetitions and Applications of the Senses. After I have finished contemplating the Passion in this way, we could spend one more day just letting the Passion in its whole sweep pervade our day. In all these suggested approaches, the good progress of the retreat is always the prime consideration.

GUIDELINES WITH REGARD TO EATING, [210]

Preliminary Note: As a person begins to grow in his knowledge of Jesus Christ and union with him through the exercises of the Second and Third Weeks, it is clear that the "sense of Christ" is meant to permeate his whole being and all his activities. To reflect on the daily and commonplace activity of eating is to emphasize how total is my response to follow Jesus Christ. As St. Paul says, "whether you eat or drink--whatever you do--you should do all for the glory of God." (1 Cor 10:31)

The following guidelines, then, are meant to model a reflective approach about my conduct in every part of my life so that being ever more fully penetrated by the life of Christ within me, I show forth a proper ordering in the various areas of my life. In the words of St. Paul, "whatever you do, work at it with your whole being" (Col 3:23). Through such guidelines, I can begin even now to live out the reordering process which has begun to be effected in me during the course of the retreat.

A. General Principle

1. [214] It is while a person is eating that he should reflect upon Christ and his apostles at table. He should try to enter into the presence of Christ so fully that he can have a sense of how Jesus eats and drinks, how he speaks and handles himself in the context of a meal. Even at the very time of doing this exercise of the imagination, he will find that he no longer has the food itself as a focus of his attention. As a result, he will come to a greater order in his own conduct at table, perhaps both in what he eats and in how he acts while eating.

A Contemporary Reading of

B. Particular Applications

2, [210]. There seems to be less problem for a proper ordering
in a person's life when it is a matter of bread or the ordinary
staples of diet.

3, [211]. There does seem to be a greater care necessary when
we consider the area of drink. Whatever the beverage--beer, soda,
coffee, milk, wine, and so on--a person should consider what is helpful and so pursue the good mean for himself, and also what may be
harmful and so avoid the bad.

4, [212]. When we consider the wide variety of food available
to us, we should be more conscious of its appeal to our appetites
and so the necessity for a greater sense of control. To avoid disorder concerning foods, a certain abstinence can be practiced in two
ways:

(a) by seeking out the less delicate foods, even to a greater
    dependence on the staples within the diet;

(b) by eating sparingly of rich and delicate foods.

5, [213]. It is good to discover a proper mean for oneself in
his eating habits. While taking care not to fall sick, a person can
reduce his intake of food in order to come to such a mean. There
are two reasons why seeking such a mean can be profitable:

(a) commonly the observation of a mean in one's diet provides
    a disposition whereby a person will often experience more
    abundant lights, consolations, and divine movements within
    his spirit. These experiences, in turn, may confirm a per-
    son in the ordering of such a mean in eating.

(b) when one discovers that observing a certain chosen mean in
    diet brings about an inability to continue well in the per-
    formance of the exercises of the retreat, he will then come

more easily to adjust such a mean in order that he can
have the necessary strength and health for his ordinary
daily life and activity.

C. Particular Attitudes

6, [215]. In regard to one's attention at a meal time, a person
may find a reading about a saint or a particular spiritual apostolate
very helpful in fixing one's focus beyond the mere gratification of
one's hunger. Music, too, can provide a reflective and relaxed setting for meals.

7, [216]. If the whole focus of one's attention at meals is
upon food itself, a person can find that he is carried away by his
appetites. He may also discover that he is bolting his food so
hurriedly that there is a little evidence of a Christ-behavior in
his activity of eating a meal. Both in the amount of food eaten and
in the way it is eaten, a person should be ordering his life in
Christ.

8, [217]. If a person were to plan ahead for his meals, he may
find that an order in his eating habits is far easier to accomplish.
For example, it can be very helpful after lunch or after dinner or
at a time when one does not feel a desire for food to determine how
much he will eat at the next meal. Then at the time of the meal itself, he should not exceed that amount which he set himself, no matter how strong the temptation might be. In fact, if he finds himself
strongly moved by his appetites to eat more, he should take even less
than the amount he had predetermined.

A Contemporary Reading of

THE FOURTH WEEK

The First Day and First Contemplation:
the Appearance of Christ our Lord to Mary, 218-225]

PREPARATION: the usual preparatory reverence.

GRACE: I will beg for the gift of being able to enter into the joy
and consolation of Jesus in the victory of his risen life.

THE SETTING: In the usual way, I will try to enter into this contemplation as fully as I can. Although I do not have a Scripture
account to guide my thoughts, I can easily know the excitement of
Jesus in wanting to share the joy of his resurrection with his Mother
who had stood by him throughout the Passion. I let the delight and
love of this encounter permeate my being.

In contrast to the Passion, I should note how much the divinity
shines through the person of Christ in all his appearances. The
peace and joy which he wants to share with me can only be a gift of
God. To realize that the role of consoler which Christ performs in
each of his resurrection appearances is the same role he performs now
in my life is a faith insight into why I can live my life in a true
Christian optimism.

COLLOQUY: According to the circumstances of the setting, I let my
response be directed to one or more persons or let it be in the threefold manner to Mary, Christ, and the Father. In every case, always
close the prayer period with an Our Father.

FURTHER DIRECTIONS, [226-229]

1. In all the contemplations of this Fourth Week--the mysteries
of the Resurrection through the Ascension inclusive, the usual procedure should be followed as was done in the previous Weeks. A

shortening or lengthening of the Week can easily be made by a
selection or division of the various mysteries.

2.   Ordinarily it is more in keeping with the atmosphere of
relaxed consolation in this Week to have no more than four periods
of prayer within the day. As a result, the pattern of prayer periods
begins with the one upon arising in the morning, the second later in
the morning, the third sometime in the afternoon, and the fourth
period, which is usually described as the Application of the Senses,
in the evening.

3.   As I allow the Scripture passage to present me with the
setting for prayer, I know that certain elements provide me with a
focus. I should be sure to let these focal points direct my attention during the prayer period so that the general good feeling of
this Week with its possible distractions or scattering of attention
does not mitigate my response to the Lord.

4.   In the Fourth Week, I must make some modifications in the
helps toward making the whole day consistently prayerful.

As soon as I awake, I should recall the atmosphere of joy which
pervades this Week and review the particular mystery about which I
am to contemplate.

Throughout the day, I should try to keep myself in a mood which
is marked by happiness and spiritual joy. As a result, anything in
my environment--the sun and warm weather or the white cover of snow,
all the different beauties of nature, and so on--should be used to
reinforce the atmosphere of consolation.

Obviously, during this period, penance is not in keeping with
the total movement, and so only the usual temperance and moderation
in all things is encouraged.

A Contemporary Reading of

CONTEMPLATION ON THE LOVE OF GOD, [230-237]

Preliminary Note: Before this exercise is presented, two observations should be made:

(1) the first is that love ought to show itself in deeds over and above words;

(2) the second is that love consists in a mutual sharing of goods. For example, a lover gives and shares with the beloved something of his personal gifts or some possession which he has or is able to give; so, too, the beloved shares with the lover. In this way, one who has knowledge shares it with one who does not, and this is true for honors, riches, and so on. In love, one always wants to give to the other.

PREPARATION: I will take the usual time to place myself reverently in the presence of my Lord and my God.

GRACE: I should beg for the gift of an intimate knowledge of all the sharing of goods which God does in his love for me. Filled with gratitude, I want to be empowered to respond just as completely in my love and service of him.

THE SETTING: There are four different focal points which present the subject matter for my prayer:

1. God's gifts to me:

God creates me out of love which desires nothing more than a return of love on my part. So much does he love me that even though I take myself away from him, he continues to be my Savior and Redeemer.

All my natural abilities and gifts, along with the gifts of Baptism and the Eucharist and the special graces lavished upon me, are only so many signs of how much God our Lord shares his life with me. My consolation: who I am by the grace of God!

If I were to respond as a reasonable man, what could I give in
return to such a Lover? Moved by love, I may want to express my own
love-response in the following words:

TAKE AND RECEIVE

Take, Lord, and receive all my liberty, my memory, my
understanding, and my entire will--all that I have and
possess. You have given it all to me. To You, Lord,
I return it. Everything is yours; dispose of it according to your will. Give me only your love and your
grace. That is enough for me.

2. God's gift of himself to me:

God not only gives gifts to me, but he literally gives himself
to me. He is not only the Word in whom all things are created, but
also the Word who becomes flesh and dwells with us. He gives himself
to me so that his Body and Blood become the food and drink of my life.
He pours out upon me his Spirit so that I can cry out "Abba." God
loves me so much that I literally become a dwelling-place or a temple
of God--growing in an ever deepening realization of the image and likeness of God which remains the glory of man's creation.

If I were to make only a reasonable response, what could I do?
Moved by love, I may find that I can respond best in words like the
TAKE AND RECEIVE.

3. God's labors for me:

God loves me so much that he enters into the very struggle of
life. Like a potter with clay, like a mother in childbirth, or like
a mighty force blowing life into dead bones, God labors to share his
life and his love. His labors take him even to death on a cross in

order to bring forth the life of the resurrection.

Once more I question myself how I can make a response. Let me
look again to the expression of the TAKE AND RECEIVE.

4. God as Giver and Gift:

God's love shines down upon me like the light rays from the sun,
or his love is poured forth lavishly like a fountain spilling forth
its waters into an unending stream. Just as I see the sun in its
rays and the fountain in its waters, so God pours forth himself in
all the gifts which he showers upon me. His delight and his joy is
to be with the sons of men--to be with me. He cannot do enough to
speak out his love for me--ever calling me to a fuller and better
life.

What can I respond to such a generous Giver? Let me consider
once again the expression of the TAKE AND RECEIVE.

Close the prayer period with an Our Father.

Note,

There are a number of approaches which can be used in the application of this Contemplation on the Love of God.

The Contemplation could provide the prayer material for the final
day or days of the Fourth Week and so close out the retreat. All
four points of the Contemplation could be used in a single prayer
period. Then the repetitions would continue to simplify the response
throughout the prayer periods of the day. Perhaps one or two points
of the Contemplation might provide the material for the whole day,
with the usual repetitions being employed.

Another approach would be to use the Contemplation as a whole

or with any one of its points as the final prayer period of each
day within the Fourth Week, taking the place of the usual Application of the Senses. Perhaps one final day would be spent upon the
total material of the Contemplation, after the manner of reviewing
the whole of the Passion in Third Week.

Whatever is more conducive to the good closure of the retreat
for the particular retreatant is the determining guide for how to
proceed.

A Contemporary Reading of

SCRIPTURE TEXTS

Preliminary Note: Although St. Ignatius Loyola did not suggest any
Scripture texts during the time for considering The Foundation or
even during the First Week meditations, it is a common practice to
approach or reinforce this material through the use of Scripture.

Some suggested texts are presented for this early part of the
Exercises in a manner that is consistent with the Ignatian presentation for the Second, Third, and Fourth Weeks. The texts presented
are to be used or not, always in view of the needs of a particular
retreatant and the abilities of an individual retreat director. Different texts, as well as additional texts, are possible because the
only criterion is always the good progress of this particular retreat.

A. Some Suggested Scripture Texts for the Foundation:

1. MAN IS CREATED

> Psalm 103
>> Focus: how good God is to man.

Note: When praying a psalm, a number of approaches can be used:

   (1) very slowly reading through the psalm, making it one's
prayer expression;

   (2) letting certain lines or phrases hold one's attention for the
whole period of prayer;

   (3) thoughtfully reading through the psalm a number of times
within the prayer period.

2. GOD THE CREATOR

> Psalm 104
>> Focus: how great God is .

3. THE LORD, OUR GOD

> Psalm 105
>> Focus: how faithful God is to man.

4. GRATITUDE TO GOD

>> Psalm 136

> Focus: the mantra-like response to every thought about God--
> "For his mercy endures forever."

5. THE CREATION OF MAN

>> Genesis 1-2:4

> Focus: a good creation with man at its center.

6. THE WORD IN CREATION

>> John 1:1-14

> Focus: God's Word--the center and source of all life.

7. THE NEARNESS OF GOD

>> Psalm 139

> Focus: how well God knows me and how close he is to me.

8. GOD INVITES US

>> Isaiah 55

> Focus: God gives so freely and so effectively.

9. GOD'S DWELLING AMONG MEN

>> Revelation 21:1-8

> Focus: God is always with us in this "new earth."

10. CHRIST AS SOURCE OF ALL LIFE

>> Colossians 1:15-23

> Focus: Jesus Christ as the center of creation and our center.

11. WE MUST BE FREE TO RESPOND

>> Genesis 12:1-9 and Genesis 22: 1-18

> Focus: Abraham's faith in God's lead.

12. WE MUST BE FREE TO RESPOND

>> Acts 9:1-19

> Focus: Saul's conversion to Christ's lead.

13. WE MUST BE FREE TO RESPOND

>> Mark 10:17-31

> Focus: the following of God's call is free, but costly.

A Contemporary Reading of

B. Some Suggested Scripture Texts for the First Week:

14. THE FIRST SIN OF MAN
                    Genesis 3:1-19
        Focus: one sin and its effect.

15. THE HISTORY OF SIN
                    Psalm 106
        Focus: how many times men continue to reject a loving God.

16. REJECTION OF GOD AS REJECTION OF LIFE
                    Matthew 13:4-23
        Focus: God's seed within man must be nurtured or else death.

17. RECOGNITION OF SIN
                    2 Samuel 12:1-15
        Focus: how blind a man can be to his own actions.

18. EXPERIENCE OF SIN
                    Romans 7:13-24
        Focus: how deep the effects of sin are in man.

19. PERSONAL RESPONSIBILITY FOR SIN
                    Ezekiel 18:1-32
        Focus: "I" am responsible for my choices.

20. SIN CONFESSED BEFORE GOD
                    Isaiah 59:1-21
        Focus: as sinner, I come before my God.

21. SINNER IS WHAT I AM
                    1 John 1:5-2:17
        Focus: I am sinner and saved.

22. FORGIVENESS
                    Matthew 18:21-35
        Focus: God's forgiveness and my own.

23. JUDGMENT
                    Matthew 25:31-46
        Focus: God's actions and my own.

24. JUDGMENT
                    Matthew 7:1-23
        Focus: God's will and my own.

25. PRAYER OF A SINNER

> Psalm 38

Focus: I cry out to God in my need.

26. PRAYER OF REPENTANCE

> Psalm 51

Focus: I ask for mercy.

27. DEATH TO SIN

> Romans 6

Focus: Sin is possible, but I choose Christ.

28. THE RAISING OF LAZARUS

> John 11:1-44

Focus: one who is dead is raised up by Christ.

C. The Mysteries of the Life of Our Lord--Second Week: [261]

29. THE ANNUNCIATION TO OUR LADY [262]

> Luke 1:26-38

Focus: God's word and Mary's response.

30. THE VISITATION OF OUR LADY TO ELIZABETH [263]

> Luke 1:39-56

Focus: Mary rejoices in being the Christ-bearer.

31. BIRTH OF CHRIST OUR LORD [264]

> Luke 2:1-14

Focus: the simple gaze upon God-become-man.

32. THE SHEPHERDS [265]

> Luke 2:8-20

Focus: how the good news affects men.

33. THE CIRCUMCISION [266]

> Luke 2:21

Focus: the meaning of the name Jesus.

34. THE MAGI [267]

> Matthew 2:1-12

Focus: the great faith called forth in the Magi.

35. THE PURIFICATION OF OUR LADY AND THE PRESENTATION
OF THE CHILD JESUS [268]

> Luke 2:22-39

> Focus: the faithful examples of Mary, Jesus, Simeon,
> and Anna.

36. THE FLIGHT INTO EGYPT [269]

> Matthew 2:13-18

> Focus: the care of God's providence.

37. THE RETURN FROM EGYPT [270]

> Matthew 2:19-23

> Focus: God's work in ordinary human decisions.

38. THE LIFE OF CHRIST OUR LORD FROM THE AGE OF TWELVE TO THE
AGE OF THIRTY [271]

> Luke 2:51-52

> Focus: how ordinary is the growth of Jesus.

39. JESUS GOES UP TO THE TEMPLE AT THE AGE OF TWELVE [272]

> Luke 2:41-50

> Focus: Jesus' sense of a special call.

40. THE BAPTISM OF CHRIST [273]

> Matthew 3:13-17

> Focus: Jesus is clearly called forth by his Father.

41. THE TEMPTATION OF CHRIST [274]

> Luke 4:1-13; Matthew 4:1-11

> Focus: the reality of temptation in Christ's calling.

42. THE VOCATION OF THE APOSTLES [275]

> John 1:35-51; Luke 5:1-11; Matthew 4:18-22;
> Matthew 9:9; Mark 1:16-20

> Focus: Jesus calls in a special way to certain persons.

43. THE FIRST MIRACLE PERFORMED AT THE MARRIAGE FEAST OF
CANA IN GALILEE [276]

> John 2:1-11

> Focus: Mary's faith and Jesus' response.

44. CHRIST CASTS THE SELLERS FROM THE TEMPLE [277]

> John 2:13-22

> Focus: zeal to carry out his Father's will.

45. THE SERMON ON THE MOUNT [278]

Matthew 5

Focus: the strategy of Christ.

46. CHRIST CALMS THE STORM [279]

Matthew 8:23-27

Focus: Christ, the power of God.

47. CHRIST WALKS ON THE WATER [280]

Matthew 14:22-23

Focus: Christ's call to an ever greater faith.

48. THE APOSTLES ARE SENT TO PREACH [281]

Matthew 10:1-16

Focus: Jesus shares his mission.

49. THE CONVERSION OF MAGDALENE [282]

Luke 7:36-50

Focus: Jesus calls to conversion by love.

50. CHRIST FEEDS THE FIVE THOUSAND [283]

Matthew 14:13-21

Focus: Jesus' concern for all the people.

51. THE TRANSFIGURATION [284]

Matthew 17:1-9

Focus: Jesus' own religious experience.

52. THE RAISING OF LAZARUS [285]

John 11:1-45

Focus: Jesus as the Resurrection and the Life.

53. THE SUPPER AT BETHANY [286]

Matthew 26:6-10

Focus: Jesus' acceptance of a love gesture.

54. PALM SUNDAY [287]

Matthew 21:1-17

Focus: Jesus as King.

55. JESUS PREACHES IN THE TEMPLE [288]

Luke 19:47-48

Focus: Jesus' fidelity to his mission.

D.   The Mysteries of the Life of Our Lord--Third Week:

56.   THE LAST SUPPER [289]
                    Matthew 26:20-30; John 13:1-30
         Focus: Jesus serves in giving himself totally.

57.   FROM THE LAST SUPPER TO THE AGONY INCLUSIVE [290]
                    Matthew 26:30-46; Mark 14:32-44
         Focus: Jesus seeks only the will of his Father.

58.   FROM THE GARDEN TO THE HOUSE OF ANNAS INCLUSIVE [291]
                    Matthew 26:47-58; Luke 22:47-57; Mark 14:44-54
                       and 66-68
         Focus: Jesus lives his passion.

59.   FROM THE HOUSE OF ANNAS TO THE HOUSE OF CAIPHAS INCLUSIVE [292]
                    Matthew 26; Mark 14; Luke 22; John 18
         Focus: Jesus lives his passion.

60.   FROM THE HOUSE OF CAIPHAS TO THE HOUSE OF PILATE INCLUSIVE [293]
                    Matthew 27; Luke 23; Mark 15
         Focus: Jesus lives his passion.

61.   FROM THE HOUSE OF PILATE TO THE HOUSE OF HEROD [294]
                    Luke 23:6-11
         Focus: Jesus lives his passion.

62.   FROM THE HOUSE OF HEROD TO THAT OF PILATE [295]
                    Matthew 27; Luke 23; Mark 15; John 19
         Focus: Jesus lives his passion.

63.   FROM THE HOUSE OF PILATE TO THE CROSS INCLUSIVE [296]
                    John 19:13-22
         Focus: Jesus lives his passion.

64.   JESUS DIES UPON THE CROSS [297]
                    John 19:23-27; Matthew 27:35-52; Mark 15:24-38;
                       Luke 23:34-46
         Focus: Jesus fulfills the Father's will to the very end.

65.   FROM THE CROSS TO THE SEPULCHER INCLUSIVE [298]
                    Ibidem
         Focus: the sense of loss, emptiness, waiting.

E. The Mysteries of the Life of Our Lord--Fourth Week:

66. THE RESURRECTION OF CHRIST OUR LORD--THE FIRST APPARITION [299]

No Scripture text

Focus: Jesus in his consoling role for Mary his Mother.

67. THE SECOND APPARITION [300]

Mark 16:1-11

Focus: "He is risen."

68. THE THIRD APPARITION [301]

Matthew 28

Focus: Jesus the consoler.

69. THE FOURTH APPARITION [302]

Luke 24:9-12 and 33-34

Focus: the wonder of the resurrection.

70. THE FIFTH APPARITION [303]

Luke 24

Focus: Christ the consoler.

71. THE SIXTH APPARITION [304]

John 20:19-23

Focus: Christ the life-giver.

72. THE SEVENTH APPARITION [305]

John 20:24-29

Focus: faith in the Lord Jesus.

73. THE EIGHTH APPARITION [306]

John 21:1-17

Focus: Christ the consoler.

74. THE NINTH APPARITION [307]

Matthew 28:16-20

Focus: Christ sends out his followers.

75. THE TENTH APPARITION [308]

1 Cor 15:6

Focus: Christ the consoler.

76. THE ELEVENTH APPARITION [309]

1 Cor 15:7

Focus: Christ the consoler.

77. THE TWELFTH APPARITION: APPEARANCE TO JOSEPH OF ARIMATHEA [310]

No Scripture text

Focus: Christ the consoler.

78. THE THIRTEENTH APPARITION [311]

1 Cor 15:8

Focus: Christ as the consoler.

79. THE ASCENSION OF CHRIST OUR LORD [312]

Acts 1:1-12

Focus: Christ ever present and Christ who will come again.

GUIDELINES FOR THE DISCERNMENT OF SPIRITS, [313]

Preliminary Note: On the use of "spirits," good and evil.

"Discernment of spirits" is a venerable phrase of Christian
spiritual tradition. The word spirits used in this context might
be described as "movements of one's heart or spirit," "motions affecting one's interior life," "a certain impetus in one's life," "a
feeling for or against some course of action," and so on. The de-
scriptive words "good" and "evil" as applied to "spirits" are used to
designate primarily the kind of movement or feeling in terms of its
direction or goal. Good spirits lead a person in a good direction
towards a good goal. Evil spirits make use of evil directions and
even sometimes what are preliminarily good directions to accomplish
an evil end.

Although the importance of these movements comes in the direction
which they give to our lives, we are necessarily concerned about recog-
nizing their good or evil source, especially in view of the possible
deception of an apparently good direction. In the light of modern
psychology, we have some indications of the great complexity of human
motivations. Added to this complexity of human motivation, we Chris-
tians live in a faith-world which acknowledges the unfathomable power
of evil personified in Satan and the damned of hell and the even more
mysterious power of good focused in God and in the communion of saints.
And so when we attempt to say something not only about the direction
of these spirits but also about what the sources of these good and
evil spirits or motions are, we can still find helpful the tradi-
tional Ignatian schema:

          good spirits and evil spirits come from:
               (1) within our very selves
               (2) outside of us
                    (a) our fellow men
                    (b) power more than human.

Although as redeemed sinners we can confess that both good and
evil motives emanate from within us, we still stand amazed at both
the good and the evil which comes forth from the heart of man. Like

St. Paul in his seventh chapter of the Letter to the Romans, we suffer from the division we feel within our very selves. In fact, we
commonly feel more comfortable to be able to blame evil on someone
or something outside of ourselves. Even the first sin of man is
pictured in such a way in the third chapter of Genesis when Adam
attempts to shift the blame to Eve, and Eve looks to the serpent.
Yet without in any way lessening our own potential human malice,
we have experientially as well as scripturally the evidence of a
power of evil that is bigger than any one man or group of men.
Just as our fellowmen can influence our choices and action towards
wrong, so too the "more than human" power of evil is destructive
and deadly in its enticements and enslavements. While our fellowmen can also be an influence for good, we know similarly from experience and from scripture another power of good, which comes
from God himself directly intervening in our lives as well as the
continuing intercession of the saints who have gone before us.

In the following guidelines for discerning spirits, an attempt
is made to give helps to develop an ability to recognize ever
earlier the direction of certain movements or feelings in our
lives, and so to be able to follow or reject them almost in their
very sources.

PART I. Guidelines Suitable Especially for the First Week

The statements below are an attempt to prevent certain norms
which might be helpful in understanding different interior movements
which happen in the "heart" of man. By the grace of God, we are
meant to recognize those that are good so that we might let them give
direction to our lives and those that are bad so that we might reject them or turn aside from them.

The norms in this first section are more appropriate to the kind
of spiritual experiences associated with the First Week of the Exercises.

A. Two Statements of General Application:

1, [314]. When a person is caught up in a life of sin or perhaps even if he is closed off from God in only one area of his life, the evil spirit is ordinarily accustomed to propose a slothful complacency or a future of ever greater pleasures still to be grasped. He fills a person's imagination with all kinds of sensual delights so that there is no will or desire to change the evil direction of one's life.

The good spirit uses just the opposite method with such a person. He will try to make a person see the absurdity of the direction his life has taken. Little by little an uneasiness described sometimes as the "sting" of conscience comes about and a feeling of remorse sets in.

2, [315]. When a person is intent upon living a good life and seeking to pursue the lead of God in his life, the tactics of the spirits are just the opposite of those described above.

The evil spirit proposes to such a person all the problems and difficulties in living a good life. The evil spirit attempts to rouse a false sadness for things which will be missed, to bring about anxiety about persevering when one is so weak, to suggest innumerable roadblocks in walking the way of the Lord. And so the evil spirit tries discouragement and deception to deter a person from growing in the Christ-life.

The good spirit, however, strengthens and encourages, consoles and inspires, establishes a peace and sometimes moves to a firm resolve. To lead a good life gives delight and joy, and no obstacle seems to be so formidable that it cannot be faced and overcome. The good spirit thereby continues an upright person's progress in the Lord.

B. Particular Statements Referring Especially to Persons Intent upon Changing Their Lives and Doing Good.

First of all, two terms should be defined:

3, [316]. SPIRITUAL CONSOLATION. This term describes the interior life of a person:

(a) when he finds himself so on fire with the love of God that neither anything nor anyone presents itself in competition with a total gift of self to God in love. Rather he begins to see everything and everyone in the context of God, their Creator and Lord;

(b) when he is saddened, even to the point of tears, for his infidelity to God but at the same time thankful to know God as Savior. Such consolation often comes in a deep realization of himself as sinner before a God who loves him, or in the face of Christ's Passion when he sees that Jesus loves his Father and his fellowmen so much, or for any other reason which leads him to praise and think and serve God all the better;

(c) when he finds his life of faith, hope, and love so strengthened and emboldened that the joy of serving God is foremost in his life. A deep-down peace comes in just "being in my Father's house."

4, [317]. SPIRITUAL DESOLATION. This term describes the life of a person:

(a) when he finds himself enmeshed in a certain turmoil of spirit or feels himself weighed down by a heavy darkness or weight;

(b) when he experiences a lack of faith or hope or love in the very distaste for prayer or for any spiritual activity and he knows a certain restlessness in his carrying on in the service of God;

(c) when he experiences just the opposite effect of what has been described as spiritual consolation. For he will notice that the thoughts of rebelliousness, despair, or selfishness which arise at the time of desolation are in absolute contrast with the thoughts of the praise and service of God which flow during the time of consolation.

Four guidelines dealing with spiritual desolation now follow:

5, [318]. When we find ourselves weighed down by a certain desolation, we should not try to change a previous decision or to come to a new decision. The reason is that in desolation the evil spirit is making an attempt to obstruct the good direction of our life or to change it, and so we would be thwarted from the gentle lead of God, and what is more conducive to our own salvation. As a result, at a time of desolation, we hold fast to the decision which guided us during the time before the desolation came on us.

6, [319]. Although we should not try to make new decisions at a time of desolation, we should not just sit back and do nothing. We are meant to fight off whatever is making us less than we should be. And so we might try to intensify our prayer, we might take on some penance, or we might make a closer examination of ourselves and our life of faith.

7, [320]. Oftentimes in desolation, we feel that God has left us to fend for ourselves. By faith we know that he is always with us in the strength and power of his grace, but at the time of apparent abandonment we are little aware of his care and concern. We experience neither the support or the sweetness of his love, and our own response lacks fervor and intensity. It is as if we are living a skeletal life of the bare bones of faith.

8, [321]. The important attitude to nourish at a time of desolation is patience. Patience can mitigate the frustration, dryness, or emptiness of the desolation period and so allow us to live through it a little less painfully. We should try to recall that everything has its time, and consolation has been ours in the past and will be God's

gift in the future. Patience should mark even the efforts we under-
take to work against the desolation which afflicts us.

9, [322]. Three important reasons why we suffer desolation are:

(1) it is our own fault because we have not lived our life
of faith with any effort. We have become tepid and slothful and our
very shallowness in the spiritual life has brought about the experience of desolation;

(2) it is a trial period allowed by God. We find ourselves
tested whether we love God or just love his gifts, whether we continue to follow his call in darkness and dryness as well as in light
and consolation;

(3) it is a time when God lets us experience our own poverty
and need. We see more clearly the free gift of consolation is not
something we can control, buy, or make our own.

Next follow two guidelines dealing with spiritual consolation:

10, [323]. When a person is enjoying a consolation period, he
should use foresight and savor the strength of such a period against
the time when he may no longer find himself in consolation.

11, [324]. A time of consolation should provide the opportunity
for a growth in true humility. A person can acknowledge with gratitude the gifts he has received and recognize the full gratuity of God's
favor. It may be well to take stock how poorly he fares when such
consolation is withdrawn.

On the other hand, if a person is afflicted by desolation, he
should take some consolation in knowing that God's grace is always
sufficient to follow the way of the Lord.

Through three images we can understand better the ways in which the evil spirit works:

12, [325]. The evil spirit often behaves like a spoiled child. If a person is firm with such a child, the child gives up his petulant ways. But if a person shows indulgence or weakness in any way, the child is merciless in wheedling his own way by stomping his feest or by false displays of affection. So our tactics must include firmness in dealing with the evil spirit in our lives.

13, [326]. The evil spirit's behavior can also be compared to a false lover. The false lover uses other people for his own selfish ends, and so he uses people like objects at his disposal or as his playthings for entertainments and good times. He usually suggests that the so-called intimacy of the relationship be kept secret because he is afraid that his duplicity will become known. So the evil spirit often acts in order to keep his own suggestions and temptations secret, and our tactics must be to bring out into the light of day such suggestions and temptations to our confessor or director or superior.

14, [327]. The evil spirit can also work like a shrewd army commander, who carefully maps out the tactics of attack at weak points of the defense. He knows that weakness is found in two ways: (a) the weakness of fragility or unpreparedness, and (b) the weakness of complacent strength which is pride. The evil spirit's attacks come against us at both of these points of weakness. The first kind of weakness is less serious in that we more readily acknowledge our need and cry out for help to the Lord. The second kind is far more serious and more devastating in its effect upon us so that it is a more favored tactic of the evil spirit.

PART II. Guidelines Suitable Especially for the Second Week

[328]. The following statements are meant to be helpful in understanding the interior movements which are a part of our spiritual

lives. These guidelines are more subtle than the norms described in
PART I because commonly in the progress of a good person's life the
direction of all movements appears to be towards God and the proper
development of one's spiritual life. These norms are especially
helpful when a person experiences certain movements which are similar
to those which are common to persons engaged in the Second Week of
the Exercises or thereafter.

A. A Statement of General Application:

1, [329]. When a good person is trying to follow the call of
the Lord in his life, he will find that the good spirit tends to give
support, encouragement, and oftentimes even a certain delight in all
his endeavors.

The evil spirit generally acts to bring about the opposite
reaction. The evil spirit will subtly arouse a dissatisfaction with
one's own efforts, will raise up doubts and anxieties about God's
love or his own response, or sting the conscience with thoughts of
pride in his attempt to lead a good life.

B. Particular Statements about Consolation:

First, consolation is described in terms of its sources:

2, [330]. God alone can bring about consolation without any con-
comitant causes. We know the experience of having certain thoughts,
achievements, or events which bring about a feeling of great consolation in our lives. We also know the effect of another person or persons whose very presence or conversation can give us joy. But we can
more readily attribute our consolation directly to the touch of God
when there is no thought, no event, no person--in general, no object
of any sort--which seems to be the source of such a movement. The
directness of sense words, such as "a touch" or "a taste," seem to
point more accurately the way to describe this special action of God
in our lives. The effect of such a taste or touch, which may bring
along delight or joy, is what we can more readily grasp and speak

about. But in these cases, we should be aware that God is truly
said to be the direct source of all our consolation.

3, [331]. When there is a reason for consolation, whether it
be from certain thoughts or achievements or events, or even more so
certain people who have an effect upon us, then either the good spirit
or the evil spirit can be involved. On the one hand, the good spirit
brings about such consolation in order to strengthen and speed the
progress of our life in Christ. The evil spirit, on the contrary,
arouses good feelings so that we are drawn to focus our attention on
wrong things, or to pursue a more selfish motivation, or to find our
own will before all else. Quietly and slowly the change is brought
about until the evil direction becomes clear.

Ways of working with spurious consolation are:

4, [332]. For a person striving to lead a good life, the evil
spirit ordinarily begins like an angel of light. For example, we
find ourselves inspired by pious thoughts or holy desires, and then
after some time we are caught up in the pride of our own intellect
and in the selfishness of our own desires.

5, [333]. We can become discerning persons by examining carefully our own experiences. If in reflecting on the course of our
thoughts or our actions we find that from beginning to end our eyes
have remained fixed on the Lord, we can be sure that the good spirit
has been moving us. But if what started off well in our thought and
action begins to be self-focused or to turn us from our way to God,
we should suspect that the evil spirit has somehow twisted the good
beginning to an evil direction, and possibly even to an evil end.
So we can discover that an original good course has led us to be
weakened spiritually or even to become desolate or confused. The
signs of desolation give clear indication of the evil spirit's influence.

6, [334]. When we recognize that we have been duped by the evil
spirit through a certain thought progression or course of action, we

should review carefully all the stages which we passed through from
the time when the evil became apparent back to its very beginnings in
the good. By means of such a review, we will find that we can more
quickly catch ourselves when we are being led on by the deceit of the
evil spirit and so we are more enabled to guard ourselves in the future.

Finally, there are further insights in regard to consolation
in the progress of one's spiritual life:

7, [335]. As a person continues to make progress in the spiritual life, the movement of the good spirit is very delicate, gentle,
and often delightful. It may be compared to the way a drop of water
penetrates a sponge.

When the evil spirit tries to interrupt the progress of such
a person, the movement is violent, disturbing, and confusing. It
may be compared to the way a waterfall hits a stone ledge below.

In persons whose lives are going from bad to worse, the descriptions given above should just be reversed. The reason for this lies
in the conflict of opposing forces. In other words, when good or
evil spirits find the heart of man a true haven, they enter quietly
just as anyone comes into his own home. By contrast, evil spirits
cause great commotion and noise as they try to enter into the heart
of the just man intent upon the good.

8, [336]. When the consolation experience in one's life comes
directly from God, there can be no deception in it. Although a delight and peace will be found in such an experience, a spiritual person should be very careful to distinguish the actual moment of this
consolation-in-God-himself from the afterglow which may be exhilarating
and joyful for some period of time. Quite often it is in this second
period of time, that a person begins to reason out plans of action or
to make resolutions which cannot be attributed so directly to God as

the initial experience which is non-conceptual in nature. Because
human reasoning and other influences are now coming into the total
picture of this consolation period, a very careful process of discerning the good and evil spirits should be undertaken according to
the previous guidelines before any resolution or plan of action is
adopted.

This table indicates where sections or paragraphs of St. Ignatius'
text are treated in this book, A Companion.

For example, Spiritual Exercises, paragraph or number [2], is treated
in the Companion, page 6; SpEx, [6] on Companion, page 6; SpEx, [65] on
Companion, page 19; and so on. See also the footnote on page 3 above.
Not quite every paragraph of St. Igantius' text is treated in the Companion.

SpEx Comp.